WHAT THE EXPERTS ARE SAYING:

"McGoey's incisive analysis of premise security litigation should be mandatory reading for anyone involved with security management. I would strongly recommend his text for security, business administration, insurance and risk management curricula."
—**Ira S. Somerson, CPP**
President, ASIS Foundation
American Society for Industrial Security

"Well written, well organized, this book will make a valuable addition to every working investigator's library."
—**George E. Posner, CLI, CPI**
Exec. Director, Calif. Assn. of Licensed Investigators

"A timely and well organized book. This book will help the attorney and security professional take a comprehensive approach to the complex area of private security and premises liability litigation. A 'must' for anyone seriously involved in lawsuits of this nature."
—**Daniel B. Kennedy, Ph.D., CPP, Professor & Chairman**
Dept. of Criminal Justice and Security Administration
University of Detroit

"An intelligent, important guide to an area of great concern to security professionals. A valuable reference book for every security library."
—**James S. Cawood, CPP, Chapter Chairman**
American Society for Industrial Security

"Chris McGoey has rendered a service to the legal profession. His lucid exposition on a complex subject will become the 'bible' for cases in this area."
—**Jack Fink**
Alameda County, Criminal Justice Committee

SECURITY
ADEQUATE ... OR NOT ?

THE COMPLETE GUIDE TO
PREMISES LIABILITY LITIGATION

Chris E. McGoey, CPP

**AEGIS
BOOKS**
Oakland, California

AEGIS
BOOKS

P.O. Box 3239
Oakland, CA 94609-0239 USA
(415) 652-5000

Copyright © 1990 by Chris E. McGoey

Library of Congress Cataloging in Publication Data

McGoey, Chris E.
Security: Adequate...Or Not ?
The Complete Guide to Premises Liability Litigation
Bibliography: p. 207
Includes Index.

1. Evidence, expert—Witness. 2. Criminal Liability—Proximate Cause—Torts. 3. Torts—Liability—Personal injuries. 4. Torts—Liability—For Criminal Acts. 5. Crime Prevention Surveys—Security Measures. 6. Law—United States. I. Title. II. McGoey, Chris E.

KF1287.5   1990   346.03   89-85169
ISBN 0-9623543-0-9 Softcover

Printed in the United States of America

Dedicated to all my colleagues and friends who have shared their knowledge along the way.

DISCLAIMER

This book was written to provide information to those interested in the subjects of security, liability, and litigation. It is sold with the understanding that the publisher and author are not engaged in the practice of law nor are they rendering legal advice. If legal or other expert assistance is required, the services of competent and licensed professionals should be sought.

The information in this book is distributed on an "as is" basis, without warranty. Neither the author nor the publisher shall have any liability to any person or entity with respect to any liability, loss, or damage caused or alleged to be caused directly or indirectly by the information contained in this book.

It is not the intent of this book to reprint all the information that is otherwise available but to complement and supplement other texts. For more information, see the many references available in the Bibliography and in the Appendix.

Every effort has been made to make this book as complete and accurate as possible. However, **there may be errors**, both typographical and in content. Therefore, this book should be used only as a general guide and not as the ultimate source of premises liability litigation information. Furthermore, the book does not reflect research of all the laws for each state and for every circumstance and contains information available only up to the printing date.

ACKNOWLEDGEMENT

We would like to thank all those who collaborated with us to make this book possible.

We are grateful to **Lou-Anne Fauteck** of Aegis Books who worked many hours editing and rewriting and also for creating the artwork for the cover.

We are also grateful to our former legal assistant, **Peter Swann**, now law student and future 'super' lawyer. He provided most of the legal research and writing for the second and third chapters as well as assisted the author with the original concept for this book.

We are indebted to our technical reviewers:

Angela Bradstreet, Esq.—Defense attorney, Carroll, Burdick, & McDonough—San Francisco, CA

Jim Cawood, CPP, CPI—Security expert & investigator—San Leandro, CA

Jack Fink—Criminal Justice Committee—Alameda, CA

J. Gary Gwilliam, Esq.—Plaintiff attorney, Gwilliam & Ivary—Oakland, CA

David Hicks, Esq.—Plaintiff attorney, Hicks & Associates Emeryville, CA

Dan Kennedy, Ph.D, CPP—Professor & security expert—Detroit, MI

David Lynch, Esq.—Defense attorney, Low, Ball & Lynch—San Francisco, CA

George Posner, CLI, CPI—Legal investigator–Albany, CA

Chuck Sennewald, CPP—Security expert–Escondido, CA

Ira Somerson, CPP—Security expert–King of Prussia, PA

Special thanks to **Dan Poynter** of Para Publishing in Santa Barbara, CA, for his expert advise on publishing and for giving us the courage to produce this book.

And thanks to **David Brostoff** & Associates in Berkeley, CA, for producing the cover mechanical and for design and marketing guidance.

We sincerely thank all these fine people and know they are proud of their contribution to this work.

ABOUT THE AUTHOR

Chris E. McGoey is an independent security consultant operating in Oakland, California. He has more than 17 years of practical experience, including over 4000 security surveys. He has designed security programs for such large national corporations as K-Mart, 7-Eleven, and Neiman-Marcus. He was instrumental in developing the 7-Eleven robbery and crime prevention programs which are recognized industry standards.

He has lectured extensively on security and crime prevention across the United States and has appeared on numerous radio and television talk shows. He was recognized by the former Governor for the State of Nevada for signification contribution to crime prevention within the state.

Mr. McGoey's academic degrees are in police science and criminal justice administration. He has been designated a Certified Protection Professional (CPP) by the American Society of Industrial Security. He is a member of the International Association of Professional Security Consultants and currently elected to their board of directors.

As a nationally acknowledged authority and a court qualified expert witness, Mr. McGoey specializes in cases where security is alleged to be negligent or inadequate.

TABLE OF CONTENTS

TABLE OF CONTENTS

SECTION 4: ADEQUACY OF SECURITY

SECTION 5: TRIAL PREPARATION

SECTION 6: APPENDICES

Lawsuits alleging inadequate security are being filed more often than ever before. Jury awards of over a million dollars are no longer exceptional. Property and business owners fear being sued and often do not have the experience to know what can be done to reduce their exposure. Security professionals sometimes feel stymied by not knowing beforehand what security measures a jury will deem adequate should their companies be sued.

Legal journals have addressed the fine points of the law, but none have touched on how to evaluate the complex security issues. Most attorneys have never accepted a premises liability lawsuit of this nature, and if one is thrust upon them many will have to learn during trial.

This book was written to serve both as an introduction for concerned property and business owners and as a practical guide for trial lawyers and security professionals. For the benefit of attorney's, step-by-step guidelines and tested formulas were written to aid in developing the concepts necessary to prepare a case.

The Appendix contains sample voir dire and interrogatory questions, written from a security expert's viewpoint, as well as a useful discovery list and other valuable resources.

It is hoped that after reading this book, each property and business owner will make a new examination of any areas at risk and take the necessary steps to increase the safety of all who come onto their property.

The author invites your comments and looks forward to including them in future editions.

Write to:

AEGIS BOOKS
P.O. Box 3239
Oakland, CA 94609-0239
(415) 652-5000
FAX (415) 655-3734.

Or contact the author directly:

Chris E. McGoey, CPP
McGoey Security Consulting
P.O. Box 3653
Oakland, CA 94609-0653
(415) 428-9155

—Chris E. McGoey, CPP

INTRODUCTION

CHAPTER ONE

Security & Premises Liability

Consider the following crimes:

1. A ten year old girl is abducted from a public sidewalk, dragged into an apartment building, and raped in a vacant unit.

2. A man and his son are assaulted in the parking lot of the apartment building in which they reside, and sustain serious physical injuries.

3. Twenty-one customers in a fast-food restaurant are killed and eleven wounded in an attack by a gunman.

4. A man is taken hostage by a robber during a convenience store holdup. While struggling with the robber inside the store, he is shot.

The scenarios above are taken from actual cases heard in courts in different states across the country, in which the victim sued the owner or occupier of the property where the crime occurred. The process that determines why victims prevail in some of these cases and not in others is the focus of this book.

Introduction

Property owners and business operators have recently become subject to what appears to be a legal trend of increasing liability for crimes committed on their premises. Historically at common law, a business owner or operator generally was not liable for injuries inflicted on a patron by an unknown assailant. Liability for the landowner could only be based on an act of negligence, with the possible exception of innkeepers, who have long been recognized by the common law to have a duty to protect their guests from harm.

Under common law, and in a few states today, liability will not be imposed even for a negligent act of a landowner, if the victim is not on the premises for business purposes. It is thus possible in such states for a landowner who injures a social guest and a business invitee on his land to be subject to liability only to the latter victim.

Over the past twenty-five years, the reported crime rate has more than tripled in America. Violent crimes have affected almost every facet of the business community: the hotel and motel industries, apartment and rental housing, shopping centers, department stores, convenience stores and fast food outlets, restaurants, parking lots, and other public gathering places.

Injuries inflicted on patrons in these public places have generated a series of cases which have expanded the theory of liability to include property owners as having a legal duty to protect land entrants from harm. There are still a few states whose courts have refused to assign a duty of care in third party criminal assault cases, and still others that are considered limited duty states. However, more and more states are converted as new cases are adjudicated.

This shift toward increased liability and the rise in violent crime have brought about a wave of personal injury litigation as the result of criminal assaults by third parties. Multimillion dollar jury verdicts have attracted the attention of the media, fueling the litigation fire.

The first major award for an inadequate security claim was reported in 1965 for $25,000. By 1982, the average jury award involving inadequate or negligent security cases had risen to $921,696.

One of the most highly publicized cases attracting attention to this type of lawsuit was that of entertainer Connie Francis, who was awarded 2.7 million dollars as the result of being raped in a Howard Johnson's Motor Lodge in 1974. The assailant gained entry to her room through a sliding glass door that was deemed inadequately secured.[1]

Over half of the states had never had a major jury award for an inadequate security case prior to 1982.[2] Ten years ago, few plaintiff attorneys would accept a premises liability case based solely on a third party criminal assault.

Most lawyers lacked the experience to take on such a case. Issues of crime foreseeability and the standard of care for security were somewhat foreign concepts and often viewed as fatal liability issues by many courts.

As we enter the 1990's, most trial lawyers still have not experienced a premises liability case involving security issues. Even though there are now articles written on the subject and a substantial body of legal precedent, there remains a large gap in understanding the issues of premises liability cases where inadequate security is the alleged cause of an injury.

Purpose of This Book

This book was written in an attempt to contribute something of value to the current approaches to the factual development of adequacy of security cases. The concepts of crime foreseeability and adequacy of security are foreign to most attorneys, security professionals, and especially to defendant landowners.

Most previous articles on premises liability litigation have been written by attorneys who have expounded on the many legal issues involved and on practice pointers to be used at trial. Very little has been written on how to evaluate and analyze the important liability issues of crime foreseeability, adequacy of security, and standards of care from a security expert's perspective.

This book was also written as a means to supply practical information to the security professional and the business community in the hope that steps would be taken to avoid injury to patrons and involvement in this type of lawsuit. This book should be of great interest to those who open their land or business to the general public.

Many business owners are frustrated by the pressure placed upon them to operate their business safely. The costs of providing for security can be enormous. Thousands of dollars can be spent on security measures that do not address the liability issues. This book may help strip away some of that fear of the unknown and allow for an affirmative action plan for providing adequate security.

The information and concepts discussed throughout this book are presented from the viewpoint of a court qualified security expert, who has been involved with the issues in premises liability litigation for more than seventeen years. The methods described by the author are practical, from having "been there" and from having to manage and operate security programs within budget.

As a means of introduction to the liability issues involved in common negligence litigation, we will briefly review the elements of a premises liability litigation.

Elements of an Adequacy of Security Claim

Most premises liability litigation involves negligence issues. At the beginning of this chapter, four scenarios were outlined that resulted in negligence lawsuits against a landowner. While the arguments presented in these specific cases will vary widely, there are five elements that generally must be proven when inadequate security is alleged against a landowner in a tort negligence action.

Simply stated they are: (1) the owner or occupier of the land owed a legal duty of care to the plaintiff; (2) assaultive crime was foreseeable on the premises; (3) the owner or occupier failed (negligence) to conform to a reasonable standard of care (protection); (4) the negligence was the proximate cause of the assault upon the plaintiff; and (5) the plaintiff was damaged (injured) as a result of that breach of duty.

Proximate cause and breach of duty may be found to exist independently, but a finding of both is required for the plaintiff to prevail. It is not sufficient for a plaintiff to show that a land possessor failed to take protective measures required of him by the law if this failure had little to do with the actual crime. Nor will it be sufficient for the plaintiff to show that the land possessor's actions were closely tied to the crime if the land possessor was under no duty to guard against it.

The question of the existence of a duty in a negligence action is a question of law, whereas the issue of proximate cause is a determination of fact usually left to the jury. These legal concepts will be reviewed in subsequent chapters in greater detail.

Organization of This Book

This book has been organized into sections to allow for individual focus on each issue.

Section Two focuses on the legal aspect of premises liability litigation and will be of greatest interest to attorneys and security professionals. However, lay persons will also benefit by learning some of the legal concepts and terminologies used in the process. Case summaries are used to illustrate and guide one through the legal concepts of legal duty and foreseeability.

Section Three of this book will focus on the concept of crime foreseeability in greater detail. A model of foreseeability is presented in Chapter Four and then examined as components in Chapters Five through Seven. It is recommended that one read these chapters in numerical order the first time through. Certain new concepts and terms are introduced in each chapter, which will aid in understanding later discussions.

Section Four discusses the more practical aspect of evaluating physical security, after first establishing important criteria for the evaluation of adequacy. Security consultants, security directors, premises operators, and attorneys should find this information valuable for conducting their own evaluations, based on the methodology outlined in Chapters Eight through Ten.

Section Five discusses the trial preparation phase in Chapter Eleven and reviews what type of information is normally requested during the discovery period by the opposing parties. It is hoped that this information will alert business operators on what documentation and procedures should be maintained for defense of a lawsuit. A discovery checklist has been supplied in the Appendix to supplement this chapter.

The final Chapter, Twelve, will discuss an effective method of presenting the highly complex issues of crime foreseeability and security to a jury.

If the concepts and methods outlined in this book are applied in litigation, an attorney will be able to present a case to a jury based on supportable facts, a supportable crime foreseeability level, and a site survey evaluation consistent with accepted professional security industry methods.

If this occurs, the book has achieved its intended goal.

Endnotes

1. *Garzilli v. Howard Johnson's Motor Lodges, Inc.*, 419 F.Supp. 1210 (1976).
2. Lawrence W. Sherman, *Protecting Customers from Crime, Draft Standards With Commentary* (Washington, D. C.: Security Law Institute, 1984), 12-13, quoting Lawrence W. Sherman, and Jody Klein, *Major Lawsuits Over Crime and Security: Trends and Patterns, 1958-82* (College Park, Md.: Institute of Criminal Justice and Criminology, University of Maryland, 1984).

LEGAL
ASPECTS

CHAPTER TWO

Trends in the Law: Duty

Historically, one major problem facing plaintiffs in premises liability litigation has been the reluctance of the common law to impose any sort of affirmative duty of protection on landowners. It has always been the duty of all persons to act reasonably, yet if no duty of protection exists, it becomes difficult to imagine a case in which a landowner can be found negligent absent willful misconduct. Without the sympathy of judges toward arguments aimed at imposing a higher, broader duty, victims were left with no theory on which to base a claim against the landowners.

Over the past two decades, many states have tended to place a greater duty upon landowners, while others have refused to expand common law negligence. As of the date of this writing, several states still maintain a policy of imposing only a limited duty or no duty whatsoever upon a landowner.

Another problem has been that a finding of proximate cause required that the landowner's alleged negligence be shown to have produced the injury in "a natural and continuous sequence, unbroken by any efficient intervening cause, ...without which the result would not have occurred."[1] Clearly, the violent act of the criminal could easily be seen as an independent cause without which the harm would never have occurred, and the negligence of the landowner could be regarded as not even a concurrent cause, eliminating the possibility of a finding of proximate cause. This line of reasoning has often convinced judges to render summary judgment in favor of the defendant but it has had varying success on appeal. The opposing line of reasoning was expressed in the Restatement of Torts:

> "The happening of the very event, the likelihood of which makes the actor's conduct negligent and so subjects the actor to liability, cannot relieve him from liability."[2]

The arguments surrounding this problem will be discussed in the context of specific cases.

The topic of the development of the tort, then, goes beyond the simple fact of the recent increase in litigation and the variety of circumstances that give rise to it. This chapter will attempt to extract the major elements of the increasingly refined definitions of duty and proximate cause, elements that fuel the arguments by which judges in various jurisdictions both expand and restrict the ability of victims to prevail against landowners for damages resulting from the criminal acts of third parties.

Defining the Duty

In describing the duty imposed upon a landowner in a given jurisdiction, four questions arise: (1) to whom is the duty owed? (2) on which parts of the property is the duty owed? (3) what positive measures are required to meet the duty? and (4) how is the required level of precaution related to the remoteness of the possibility of criminal acts on the property?

A common thread in those jurisdictions that readily impose a duty and those that do not is a focus on the relationship between the owner (or possessor) of the land and the victim of the crime. Among the special relationships considered in this type of lawsuit are those between landlord and tenant, business and customer, innkeeper and guest, and landowner and trespasser.

The California Court of Appeal provided a clear explanation of the role of relationship in assessing a duty when it quoted the Restatement of Torts in *Lopez v. McDonald's*:

> One will not be held liable for failing to control third-party conduct or to warn those who may be endangered by that conduct, unless "(a) a special relationship exists between the actor and the third person which imposes a duty on the actor to control the third person's conduct, or (b) a special relationship exists between the actor and the other which gives the other a right to protection."[3]

Section 314 of the Restatement of Torts specifically lists common carriers, innkeepers, and landowners who invite the public onto their premises for business purposes as parties engaged in the type of special relationship that creates a duty of care. Comment b of section 314A, however, makes it plain that this list is not to be considered exclusive. Witkin's analysis of this section suggests that it "refers to such additional relationships as...a person who is required by law to take, or who voluntarily takes, custody of another under circumstances that deprive the other of his normal opportunities for protection."[4]

In *Waters v. New York City Housing Authority*, the New York Supreme Court, Appellate Division also emphasized the importance of the existence of a relationship in such cases.

> To sustain the plaintiffs' claim...is to set the groundwork for dangerous precedent, i.e., that property owners who fail to secure their property with locks do so at their peril and risk liability to anyone injured thereby, regardless of the relationship.[5]

Premises liability cases in various jurisdictions have produced vastly different holdings with regard to the duty implicit in the landlord-tenant relationship. The long standing rule in Illinois, affirmed as recently as 1983,[6] is that the relationship between landlord and tenant is not the type that gives rise to a duty to protect against criminal acts of third parties, including other tenants.

In *C.S. v. Sophir*, the Supreme Court of Nebraska refused to acknowledge or deny the existence of a general duty, but rather deemed it "a question of fairness."

The test of "fairness" was expressed by the court as follows:

> Factors to consider in imposing a duty on a landlord include weighing the relationship of the parties against the nature of the risk and the public interest in the proposed solution...as well as the likelihood of injury, the magnitude of the burden of guarding against it and the consequences of placing that burden on a defendant.[7]

The court did, however, affirm the principle that landlords are not insurers that tenants will be protected at all times.[8]

The landmark case in which the immunity of an apartment landlord to this duty was first rejected was *Kline v. 1500 Massachusetts Avenue Apartment Corporation.* In its decision, the court enumerated the reasons behind the general rule that had maintained that a private person does not have a duty to protect others against criminal attack, and thereby the focal points of an inquiry into the nature of the duties that form the basis of this type of lawsuit.

> Among the reasons for the application of this rule to landlords are: judicial reluctance to tamper with the traditional common law concept of the landlord-tenant relationship; the notion that the act of a third person in committing an intentional tort or crime is a superseding cause of the harm to another resulting therefrom; the oftentimes difficult problem of determining foreseeability of criminal acts; the vagueness of the standard that the landlord must meet; the economic consequences of the imposition of the duty; and

conflict with the public policy allocating the duty of protecting citizens from criminal acts to the government rather than the private sector.[9]

The court then swept aside the determinative force of these considerations when it held:

The rationale of the general rule exonerating a third party from any duty to protect against a criminal attack has no applicability to the landlord-tenant relationship in multiple dwelling houses.

and:

The landlord is no insurer of his tenants' safety, but he is certainly no bystander....it does not seem unfair to place upon the landlord a duty to take those steps which are within his power to minimize the predictable risk to his tenants.[10] [Emphasis added.]

The general principle on which a relationship could be held to result in a duty was expressed as an extension of the reasoning behind the more commonly recognized duties inherent in those relationships such as employer-employee, hospital-patient and carrier-passenger:

In all, the theory of liability is essentially the same: that since the ability of one of the parties to provide for his own protection has been limited in some way by his submission to the control of the other, a duty should be imposed on the one possessing control (and thus the power to act) to take reasonable precautions to protect the other one from assaults by third parties which, at least, could reasonably have been anticipated.[11]

Seven years later, the California Court of Appeal followed the *Kline* decision. It held in *O'Hara v. Western Seven Trees Corporation Intercoast Management*[12] and later in *Kwaitkowski v. Superior Trading Co.*[13] that the relationship between landlord and tenant was a special one, which, combined with the implied warranty of habitability and the foreseeability of criminal attack, formed the basis for a duty to exercise reasonable care.

Quite recently, condominium owner associations have been held to the same duty of care as landlords to protect residents from criminal acts of third parties. Courts in Hawaii and California have based this extension of the duty on the similarity between the functions of these entities and on the fact that each has exclusive control over the common areas on a given facility. *Moody v. Cawdrey & Associates*[14] and *Frances T. v. Village Green Owners Association*[15] expanded the duty to include liability for failure to protect against criminal assaults as well as physical defects.

Both relied on the expression of the analogy found in *O'Connor v. Village Green Owners Association*:[16]

> "In brief, the association performs all the customary business functions which in the traditional landlord-tenant relationship rest on the landlord's shoulders."[17]

Across the country, the duty incumbent upon a business to exercise care to protect those on the premises for business purposes has been much more readily recognized than that of a landlord. Even in Illinois, the court grudgingly acknowledged that the owners of shopping malls may have a duty to protect their customers.

> where there are factual allegations indicating an awareness on the part of the owners or operators of a history of assaults in the parking facilities provided to business invitees...or where the facts suggest notice that the area is frequented by undesirable characters... liability may arise.[18]

The Supreme Court of Nebraska stated this principle more strongly *in dicta* in *C.S. v. Sophir.*

> A possessor of land who holds it open for public entry for business purposes is under a duty to exercise reasonable care to protect his patrons. Such care may require giving warning or providing greater protection where there is a likelihood that third persons will endanger the safety of the visitors.[19]

The relative importance of the element of reasonable foreseeability in the assessment of the duty was also emphasized by the California Court of Appeal in 1987.

> The special relationship between a business establishment and its customers as a matter of law places an affirmative "duty" on the

proprietor to take reasonable precautions against *reasonably anticipative* criminal conduct of unknown third parties.[20]

Public facilities such as transit systems and schools have also been found to owe a duty of protection. The Third Circuit relied on the Restatement's formulation of the principle that the duty owed by a utility is greater than that owed by a business:

> "It may not be enough for the servants of the public utility to give a warning, which might be sufficient if it were merely a possessor holding its land open to the public for its private business purposes."[21]

The court then added:

> A utility may be required to take additional steps to control the conduct of third persons or otherwise protect the patron against it.[22]

The California courts [*Rodriguez v. Inglewood Unified School District*[23]] have noted that the relationship between a school and its students was of the special sort that created an affirmative duty to protect against injuries caused by third parties. It was only in 1982, however, that this duty took on any real meaning in terms of liability, with the California Constitution's waiver of the state's exemption from liability and creation of a statute providing a right to safe schools.[24]

In addition, the *Rodriguez* court noted several California decisions that recognized a special relationship between the patrons and proprietors of bowling alleys, restaurants, apartment houses, and hospitals.[25]

Traditionally, where a possible duty of care in premises liability cases has been found to exist, the courts have recognized a further distinction between invitees, licensees, and trespassers. In general, a higher standard of care exists with respect to invitees (business visitors) than with regard to licensees (social guests) and trespassers. In California and many other jurisdictions, the general rule before 1968 was that an inviter owes an invitee the common law duty of ordinary care. Both social guests and trespassers were obliged to "take the premises as they found them," and the only duty owed by the possessor of the land was "refraining from wanton or willful injury."[26]

While it may at first glance seem reasonable to require trespassers to bear the risk of their presence on a property, this distinction falters in a case such as the first listed at the beginning of chapter one, in which a girl was *dragged* onto a property and raped. Should the mere fact that the victim was not a licensee or invitee of the landowner or his tenant render them immune from liability that would otherwise exist?

These were the facts in *Nixon v. Mr. Property Management Company, Inc.*. In this case, the vacant apartment in which the crime occurred had been not been maintained in accordance with an ordinance that required that doors and windows be securely closed to prevent unauthorized entry.

As mentioned above, such a violation will, in most jurisdictions, be evidence of negligence and in other jurisdictions will be negligence *per se*. The court found that since "unexcused violation of a statute or ordinance constitutes negligence as a matter of law if such statute or ordinance was designed to prevent injury to the class of persons to which the injured party belonged,"[27] the threshold question to a finding of negligence was whether the fact that the victim was technically a trespasser was determinative of the issue of duty.

The majority chose to address this question using the following line of reasoning:

> An ordinance requiring apartment owners to do their share in deterring crime is designed to prevent injury to the general public. [The victim] falls within this class. Since the ordinance was meant to protect a larger class than invitees and licensees, and since [the victim] committed no wrong in coming onto the property, these premises liability distinctions are irrelevant in our analysis.[28]

The above argument is the most recent one used to eliminate the distinctions between land entrants, and it is the one that depends to the greatest degree upon logic rather than the usual moral judgments.

The concurring opinion, for example, cites *Rowland v. Christian*, which made California the first state to eliminate the distinctions between land entrants.

> "A man's life or limb does not become less worthy of protection by the law or a loss less worthy of compensation under the law because he has come upon the land of another without permission or with permission but without a business purpose. Reasonable people do not ordinarily vary their conduct

depending on [their classification as a land entrant], and to focus on the status of the injured party as a trespasser, licensee, or invitee in order to determine the question whether the landowner has a duty of care, is contrary to our social mores and humanitarian values."[29]

The court did allow for the possibility that these categories might have a bearing on the outcome of some cases, but specified that the entrant's status by itself is no longer determinative.

The *Nixon* court later adds:

The classifications of invitee, licensee, and trespasser are judicial dinosaurs which served a purpose long ago when society's values placed great emphasis on a man's property holdings. That day is gone, and with it the public-be-damned attitude of J.P. Morgan. Today, society places a great emphasis on human safety.[30]

The extent of the spread of this doctrine is also outlined in the *Nixon* decision. To date, ten jurisdictions have held that the classifications are not determinative and that landowners are subject to a duty of ordinary care, beginning with California in 1968. These also include Hawaii, Colorado, the District of Colombia, Rhode Island, Louisiana, New Hampshire, New York, Alaska, and Texas. In addition, Minnesota, Florida, Massachusetts, Wisconsin, North Dakota, and Maine have eliminated the distinction between invitees and licensees in such cases. On the other hand, fourteen states have explicitly rejected the relaxation of these distinctions by decisions of their courts of last resort.[31]

Further, New York, which eliminated the determinative force of the classification in *Basso v. Miller*,[32] rejected the principle expressed by the *Nixon* court in *Waters v. New York City Housing Authority*. The facts in that case were similar to those in *Nixon*. A girl was abducted at knife point from the public sidewalk and forced into a New York City Housing Authority apartment building where she was sexually assaulted and robbed. The court held that the city owed no duty of care to the victim because of the lack of a relationship between the landowner and victim. While noting the authority of *Basso*, the court stated:

> It is clear that a duty of care does not devolve upon the defendant New York City Housing Authority with respect to all persons who regularly traffic the sidewalks.[33]

Whether this decision was motivated simply by government's reluctance to subject itself to liability as a matter of policy or by a true reversal of the trend exhibited in *Nixon* is unclear.

In *Totten v. More Oakland Residential Housing, Inc.*,[34] the court held that since the plaintiff was not a tenant, no special relationship had been established. The fact that, even in post-*Rowland* California, a finding of *no* duty was based partially on these classifications of land entrants illustrates the uncertain viability of a defense based on them in any jurisdiction.

The next question that arises is whether this duty extends equally to all parts of the property or is stronger in certain areas. Naturally, the answer varies from state to state. Nearly all of the relevant decisions, though, are based on the premise that the duty itself springs from the landowner's control (and the victim's lack of control) over the premises.

The *Kline* court was the first to expand upon the duty of a landlord beyond physical defects to include protecting against criminal acts of third parties over the maintenance of common areas of an apartment building.

It relied on *Levine v. Katz*:

> "It has long been well settled in this jurisdiction that, where a landlord leases separate portions of property and reserves under his own control the halls, stairs, or other parts of the property for use in common by all tenants, he has a duty to all those on the premises of legal right to use ordinary care and diligence to maintain the retained parts in a reasonably safe condition."[35]

Although the assault in *Kline* took place in the common hallway of an apartment building, the more liberal jurisdictions have extended this view to allow plaintiffs to recover from landlords for assaults committed in their apartments when the only method of entry was via the common areas. For example, the California case of *O'Hara v. Western Seven Trees Corp. Intercoast, supra*, held that it was a question for the jury whether an alleged breach of duty, with respect to common areas that the criminal must have used, was a legal cause of an assault inside an apartment.

The court said:

> Respondents claim that the fact that the assault took place inside appellant's apartment should absolve them, since she, not they, had control over that area. This fact is not determinative. Failure to take reasonable precautions to safeguard the common areas under respondents' control could have contributed substantially, as alleged, to appellant's injuries.[36]

A Florida case, *Holley v. Mt. Zion Terrace Apartments, Inc.*, *supra*, relies on *O'Hara* in reaching the same conclusion, and also cites cases from Florida, the District of Columbia, and Georgia, which held similarly.

One area in which both progressive and conservative jurisdictions have refused to expand the concept of duty is on the question of whether a landowner's voluntary protective measures can augment the duty of care. The answer appears to be that where there is no fraud or misrepresentation as to the level or type of security in place, a landowner who voluntarily takes protective measures will not be held to a higher standard of care than he would have had the measures not been in place.

In Illinois, an appellate court refused to expand the duty of a shopping mall to protect its customers from attack when it was alleged that the provision of a security force constituted a voluntary undertaking to do so.[37]

In another recent case, an Illinois Appellate court refused to deviate from the rule that a landlord owes a tenant no duty to protect him from criminal acts. In *Carrigan v. New World Enterprises, supra,* it was argued that since the landlord breached a contractual obligation to keep a burglar alarm operable, he should be held liable for harm that might have been prevented by the alarm. The court held that the undertaking to maintain the alarm did not constitute a promise to the tenant that she would be protected from criminal harm.

Even in New York, a more liberal jurisdiction in some aspects, a landlord was held liable for an assault to a tenant in the parking lot of an apartment building. The landlord had installed a lock-chain device at the entrance, and a theory of negligence was introduced on the fact that the device had failed to function. It was held improper to allow the jury to consider this fact since, in the opinion of the court, the device could not have reasonably been expected to perform the function of preventing criminal attacks.[38]

Future Trends

In California and other states, appellate courts are expanding the concept of legal duty to include adjacent properties not owned or leased by a defendant. Property owners or lessees who receive benefit from or exercise control over such adjacent property will increasingly be expected to provide the same standard of reasonable care to those who access their premises.[39]

Large national corporations and franchises with many outlets, may be held to a higher standard of foreseeability of criminal acts based on their broad experience with such activity at their other various sites.[40] For example, when forty percent of total company's outlets suffer from high crime, it becomes more difficult for that organization to state that similar crimes could not be foreseen as a possibility at other locations without crime histories.

Conclusion

It seems clear that the trend is toward an erosion of the traditional *de facto* immunity enjoyed by landowners from liability for criminal acts of third parties. It is reasonable to expect that more states will follow that trend with more liberal views on expanding the scope of the landowner's duty of care to entrants.

As the duty of providing reasonable care expands, the burden of providing security precautions will affect the way landowners conduct business in the future. Land entrants should benefit by enjoying a higher degree of safety. However, this will undoubtedly be at some increased cost and passed on to the invitee, tenant, or guest.

Endnotes

1. Henry Campbell Black, M.A., *Black's Law Dictionary, s. v.* "cause."
2. *Holley v. Mt. Zion Terrace Apartments, Inc.*, Fla.App., 382 So.2d 98 (1980), 101, quoting Rest.2d, section 449 (1965).
3. *Lopez v. McDonald's*, 238 Cal.Rptr. 436, 193 Cal.App.3d 495 (1987), 442, quoting Rest.2d Torts, section 315.
4. 4 Witkin, *Summary of Cal.Law* (8th ed. 1974) *Torts*, section 555, 2822.
5. *Waters v. New York City Hous. Auth.*, 116 A.D.2d 384, 501 N.Y.S.2d 385 (1986).
6. *Carrigan v. New World Enter., Ltd.*, 112 Ill.App.3d 970, 446 N.E.2d 265 (1985); also *Morgan v. Dalton Management Co.*, 117 Ill.App.3d 815, 454 N.E.2d 57 (1983).

7. *C.S. v. Sophir*, 368 N.W.2d 444 (Neb. 1985), 446. See syllabus by court, 445.
8. *Ibid.*, 446.
9. *Kline v. 1500 Massachusetts Avenue Apartment Corp.*, 439 F.2d 477 (D.C. Cir. 1970), 481.
10. *Ibid.*, 481.
11. *Ibid.*, 483.
12. *O'Hara v. Western Seven Trees Corp. Intercoast Management*, App., 75 Cal.App.3d 798, 42 Cal.Rptr. 487 (1978).
13. *Kwaitkowski v. Superior Trading Co.*, 123 Cal.App.3d 324, 176 Cal.Rptr. 494 (1981).
14. *Moody v. Cawdrey & Assoc.*, 721 P.2d 708 (Haw. 1986).
15. *Frances T. v. Village Green Owners Ass'*n, 723 P.2d 573, 229 Cal.Rptr. 456 (1986).
16. *O'Connor v. Village Green Owners Association*, 191 Cal.Rptr. 320.
17. *Moody, supra*, 713; and *Frances T.*, *supra*, 460, respectively.
18. *Taylor v. Hocker*, 101 Ill.App.3d 639, 57 Ill.Dec. 112, 428 N.E.2d 662, 665 (1981).
19. *C.S. v. Sophir, supra*, 447.
20. *Lopez, supra*, 441.
21. *Kenny v. Southeastern Pennsylvania Transp. Auth.*, 581 F.2d 351 (1978), 354, quoting Rest.2d Torts (1965), section 344, comment (e).
22. Ibid.
23. *Rodriguez v. Inglewood Unified School District*, 186 Cal.App.3d 707, 230 Cal.Rptr. 823 (1986).
24. *Ibid.*, 823.
25. *Ibid.*, 826.
26. *Ibid.*
27. *Nixon v. Mr. Property Management Company, Inc.*, 690 S.W.2d 546 (Tex. 1985).
28. *Ibid.*, 549.
29. *Ibid.*, 552, quoting *Rowland, supra*, 568.
30. *Ibid.*, 554.
31. *Ibid.*, 552-553.

32. *Basso v. Miller*, 40 N.Y.2d 233, 386 N.Y.S.2d 564 352 N.E.2d 863 (1976).
33. *Waters, supra.*, 387.
34. *Totten v. More Oakland Residential Hous., Inc.*, 134 Cal.Rptr. 29.
35. *Kline, supra*, 481, quoting *Levine v. Katz*, 407 F.2d 303 (1968).
36. *O'Hara, supra*, 490.
37. *Taylor, supra.*
38. *Loeser v. Nathan Hale Gardens, Inc.*, 73 A.D.2d 187, 425 N.Y.S.2d 104 (1980).
39. *Southland Corporation v. Superior Court*, 203 Cal.App.3d 656 (1988)
40. Cohen v. Southland Corporation, 157 Cal.App.3d 130, 203 Cal.Rptr. 572 (1984)

CHAPTER THREE

Trends in the Law: Foreseeability

There is substantial case law to indicate generally, based on the relationship between two parties and the location of a criminal incident, whether a landowner may owe a duty of care to a victim in a particular case. But the decisions provide little specific guidance as to the means by which we may determine whether the duty was, in fact, breached.

In all such cases in which an affirmative duty of protection is found to exist, the law requires that the landowner be found to have acted unreasonably *under the circumstances* in order for the trier of fact to determine that the duty was breached.

Probably one of the most important and difficult circumstances to evaluate is whether, in a given case, a crime was "foreseeable."

What precisely does "foreseeable" mean? And what are the actual steps that one must take in order to exercise "ordinary" or "reasonable" care? These are questions of fact, usually reserved for a jury.

In order to insure that their resolution is not left to sheer emotion or whim, it is crucial that the litigants present a clear method of evaluating them within the confines of their legal meaning.

In this chapter, we will analyze the guiding principles affecting these questions that can be derived from the case law, and the differences in these principles among jurisdictions. This will provide the foundation for a discussion of actual methods for assessing the foreseeability of crime.

The degree of foreseeability of crime has always been a factor in defining and applying a duty of care to a landowner in this type of litigation. Early cases attempted to discount the importance of the concept of foreseeability in assigning duty because it was felt that the potential for abuse was so great.

In 1970, the court in *Kline v. 1500 Massachusetts Avenue Apartment Corporation* cited *Goldberg v. Housing Authority of Newark*, in which the Supreme Court of New Jersey said:

> "Everyone can foresee the commission of crime virtually anywhere and at any time. If foreseeability itself gave rise to a duty to provide 'police' protection for others, every residential curtilage, every shop, every store, every manufacturing plant would have to be patrolled by the private arm of the owner ....Of course none of this is at all palatable."[1]

Judge Wilkey in the *Kline* opinion correctly pointed out that:

> This language seems to indicate that the [New Jersey] court was using the word *foreseeable* interchangeably with the word *possible*....It would be folly to impose liability for mere possibilities.[2]

He then went on to provide a modern definition of foreseeability in this type of tort: "we must reach the question of liability for attacks that are foreseeable in the sense that they are *probable* and predictable."[3] The court in *Kline* did recognize the "oftentimes difficult problem of determining foreseeability of criminal acts,"[4] but imposed an affirmative duty to protect against predictable risk.

It expressed the other side of its foreseeability test as follows:

> There is no liability normally imposed upon the one having the power to act if the violence is sudden and unexpected provided that the source of the violence is not an employee of the one in control.[5]

Although the Kline court attempted to lay the groundwork for a practical concept of foreseeability, controversy over both the definition and the point at which judges may rule on it as a matter of law has increased since. A California case, *Isaacs v. Huntington Memorial Hospital*, is perhaps most illustrative of the debate.

In laying out the importance of foreseeability in a finding of duty, the *Isaacs* court relied on several cases and the Restatement of Torts. Quoting *Taylor v. Centennial Bowl, Inc.* (1966), Justice Bird wrote:

It is well settled that an owner of land has a duty "to take affirmative action to control the wrongful acts of third persons which threaten invitees where the [owner][sic] has reasonable cause to anticipate such acts and the probability of injury resulting therefrom."[6]

The *Taylor* decision was written before *Rowland v. Christian*,[7] *Kline*, and others began to break down the traditional limits of landowner duty, which serves to support the theory that foreseeability is not only tied to the concept of duty, but actually a basis for it.

This principle is explained more explicitly in the *Isaacs* court's reference to the following section from the Second Restatement of Torts.

"Since the [owner of land] [sic] is not an insurer of the visitor's safety, he is ordinarily under no duty to exercise any care until he knows or has reason to know that the acts of a third person are occurring, or are about to occur. He may, however, know or have reason to know, from past experience, that there is a likelihood of conduct on the part of third persons in general which is likely to endanger the safety of the visitor, even though he has no reason to expect it on the part of a particular individual. *If the place or character of his business, or his past experience, is such that he should reasonably anticipate careless or criminal conduct on the part of third persons, either generally or at some particular time, he may be under a duty to take precautions against it, and to provide a reasonably sufficient number of servants to afford reasonable protection.*" [Italics added in *Isaacs.*][8]

To litigants in this type of case, the most frustrating aspect of foreseeability is probably that the law generally does not provide for a threshold level above which an affirmative duty applies, and below which the landowner is held merely to a duty not to injure solely through his own negligence. Rather, the level of foreseeability and the required level of precaution are taken to be variable, with the latter dependent on the former.

The section of the Restatement quoted above shows that a landowner must somehow consider the likelihood of criminal acts of third parties occurring on his property, but it does not detail the precise criteria he may use to determine whether he is actually under a heightened duty in a particular case.

The California Court of Appeal in *Gomez v. Ticor*, emphasized the balancing process outlined in *Rowland*, *supra*, and argued that foreseeability is an "elastic factor"[9]; its importance in determining whether or not a heightened duty applies actually varies with the level of foreseeability and the nature of the duty.

A basic reason put forth for this interdependency is that the law ought to reflect public policy.

The degree of foreseeability necessary to warrant the finding of a duty will thus vary from case to case. For example, in cases

> where the burden of preventing future harm
> is great, a high degree of foreseeability may
> be required....On the other hand, in cases
> where there are strong public policy reasons
> for preventing the harm, or the harm can be
> prevented by simple means, a lesser degree
> of foreseeability may be required.[10]

But having seen that foreseeability is an "elastic factor," which must usually be evaluated by a jury, we are not much closer to a clear definition of the term. How are potential litigants to approach the question of whether crime is actually, legally foreseeable? The common sense meanings vary so widely that there is no solid, intuitive starting point, and many of the judicial discussions of the subject leave one groping for a method by which we may arrive at our own evaluations.

Dictionaries provide synonyms for the verb "to foresee" such as "guess," "prophesy," and "soothsay." Webster's tells us that to foresee means to know beforehand, but specifies that the word "implies nothing about how the knowledge is derived."[11]

Indeed, the position from the *Goldberg* case quoted above, that "everyone can foresee the commission of crime virtually anywhere and at any time," is not inherently unreasonable at all.

As we examine the variety of holdings on the issue, it will become apparent that unless one already has a clear methodology for evaluating foreseeability in mind, it is quite easy to mistake current law in certain jurisdictions as adopting the *Goldberg* position.

Another normal intuitive response to the question of whether crime was foreseeable in a certain case is to attempt to assess the probability of its occurrence. This appears to be supported by the opinion in *Kline*, which used the words "probable" and "predictable."

The *Gomez* court, however, explains that:

> The California Supreme Court has recently reiterated that "'foreseeability is not to be measured by what is more probable than not, but includes whatever is likely enough in the setting of modern life that a reasonably thoughtful person would take account of it in guiding practical conduct.'"[12]

This position was also quoted by the court in *Isaacs*.

While the fact that these decisions come from different jurisdictions may help to explain some of the apparent inconsistency, it is still true that the use of an argument that attempts to assess foreseeability on a theory of probability is of uncertain value. Even in *Kline*, the seemingly less vague of the two formulations, "probability" is not a clear standard. Ordinarily, the term "probable" means that there is sufficient likelihood of an event occurring to make it reasonably expectable. But the likelihood of any particular crime happening is usually so slight that it would fail this test. It is also unlikely that the court had a specific numeric level of probability in mind as the cutoff point for legal foreseeability, and so *Kline* leaves us with little practical guidance as to when the legal duty applies.

The problems with a test based solely on probability is expressed in the dissenting opinion in *Loeser v. Nathan Hale Gardens*.

> Of course, it is foreseeable that any resident
> of New York City might at any time and in
> any place become a crime victim. Thus, a
> debate over the statistical probabilities of an
> assault on [the plaintiff's] person on the night
> under discussion serves little purpose. [13]

If this can be reasonably argued for New York City, it
is not difficult to imagine similar arguments applied to any
urban area, leaving the practical use of the test somewhat
feeble.

Both the test in *Kline* and the Restatement of Torts
indicate that foreseeability should be considered in the
context of any crime, at any time, rather than one specific
crime. While this may elevate the levels of probability from
negligible to considerable, it does nothing to provide a
clearer criterion by which the applicability of a duty can be
assessed either before an incident occurs or during litigation.

Another natural way to approach the question of
foreseeability is to look for a history of criminal incidents on
the property or in the surrounding area. In many jurisdictions, this method has been used exclusively, and has led to
the a test of foreseeability known as the "prior similars rule."

In contrast to the model presented in *Kline* this rule is
by far the least ambiguous standard by which to determine
whether a duty applies, but in the last decade it has come
under heavy fire.

Essentially, the prior similars rule holds that unless
crime of a similar nature to the one that gave rise to the
negligence action has occurred on (or in some jurisdictions
near) the property within several years prior to the incident,

the conditions of foreseeability are not met and liability cannot exist as a matter of law.

One example of an expression of the rule is found in *Wingard v. Safeway Stores, Inc.*:

> In the absence of prior similar incidents, an owner of land is not bound to anticipate the criminal activities of third persons, particularly where the wrongdoer was a complete stranger to both the landowner and the victim and where the criminal activity leading to the injury came about precipitously.[14]

Of course, there is still room for some discretion within this rule: the degree of similarity required; the remoteness in time allowed; and the distance from the property at which the prior crimes become less relevant are not clearly defined.

A Hawaii case, *Moody v. Cawdrey & Associates*, provides a discussion of the authorities on the distance from a property at which prior similar events cease to be relevant.[15] The Hawaii court cites a Maryland case in which it was held that the duty on a landlord was effective only with prior similar incidents on his own property.

> "Since the landlord can affect the risk [of personal injury or property damage from criminal activity] [sic] only within his own premises, ordinarily only criminal acts occurring on the landlord's premises, and of which he knows or should have known (and not those occurring generally in the surrounding neighborhood) constitute relevant factors in

> determining, in the particular circumstances, the reasonable measures which a landlord is under a duty to take to keep the premises safe."[16]

Two cases representative of less restrictive views of foreseeability are also mentioned. *Isaacs, supra,* explicitly rejects the prior similars rule, but holds that a relevant consideration in assessing foreseeability is whether the property is located in a high crime area. *Walkoviak v. Hilton Hotels Corp.*[17] was mentioned as taking into account whether criminal assaults occurred in close proximity to the premises.

In spite of the differences on some of the less well defined components, the prior similars rule resembles a useful standard to a far greater degree than that proposed in either *Kline* or *Gomez*, in that it provides a definite and explicit means by which foreseeability may be completely ruled out. Whether this is in fact desirable will be discussed shortly.

Courts under the prior similars rule have gone as far as to provide descriptions of specific scenarios in which the rule would deny foreseeability. In *C.S. v. Sophir,*[18] the Supreme Court of Nebraska held that where a tenant was assaulted in a dark parking lot, it would be unfair to impose a duty on a landlord based on one prior assault in the parking lot within two months. This case openly rejects the "reasonableness" test by refusing to admit foreseeability in spite of its statement that "the ordinary, reasonable person is aware or should be aware that open parking lots provide an optimum place for crime to occur."[19]

One of the practical consequences of this rule is that judges have much greater latitude in granting summary judgment than they would under a rule such as that in *Kline* or *Gomez*. The question of foreseeability is one of fact. Therefore, where the test is vague, nearly any dispute over the issue becomes a jury question, precluding summary judgment. But where the test is more specific, a judge may rule that the evidence could not reasonably be found to support a claim that crime was foreseeable, and thus that there is no triable issue of fact to present to a jury. Jurisdictions that have adopted this rule have often put forth highly stringent requirements, which eliminate most crimes from consideration. This has not surprisingly led to rather extreme defense arguments aimed at extremely restrictive interpretations of the term "similar."

For example, in *Kwaitkowski v. Superior Trading Co.*, a tenant sued her landlords when she was assaulted, robbed, and raped in the building lobby. The landlords had notice of a tenant who was assaulted and robbed two months prior, but argued that they had "no knowledge of a particular assailant and, therefore, they had 'insufficient knowledge to create a duty to defend' against the particular risk of sexual assault by a stranger."[20]

The argument that robbery and assault on the premises two months prior to a robbery, assault and rape did not meet the requirements of the prior similars rule apparently was too farfetched. The court responded by saying, "we cannot agree that simply because the prior tenant was not also raped, the landlords here should be absolved from liability" and then held that in California, "Foreseeability does not require prior identical or even similar events."[21]

Two years later the California Supreme Court argued at length in *Isaacs v. Huntington Memorial Hospital* against the validity of the prior similars rule. This case has been cited extensively in jurisdictions across the country as more and more exceptions have been carved to the rule.

The strongest criticism was argued from the standpoint of public policy as follows:

> This [prior similar] rule is fatally flawed in numerous respects. First, the rule leads to results which are contrary to public policy. The rule has the effect of discouraging land-owners from taking adequate measures to protect premises which they know are dangerous. This result contravenes the policy of preventing future harm. Moreover, under the rule, the first victim always loses, while subsequent victims are permitted recovery. Such a result is not only unfair, but is inimical to the important policy of compensating injured parties...Surely, a landowner should not get one free assault before he can be held liable for criminal acts which occur on his property.[22]

Continuing with a refutation of the entire idea that foreseeability should be equated to prior similar offenses, the court cited a prior California case in which it was held:

> "'The mere fact that a particular kind of an accident has not happened before does not...show that such accident is one which might not reasonably have been anticipated'

...Thus, the fortuitous absence of prior injury does not justify relieving defendant from responsibility for the foreseeable consequences of its acts."[23]

Moody v. Cawdrey is one of the most recent opinions dealing directly with the prior similars rule as it applies to landlords. The discussion in this case begins:

Basically, the landlord's duty to act arises after he has received notice, actual or constructive, of criminal activity either on his premises or in the immediate vicinity thereof.[24]

While this may at first appear to be an endorsement of the rule, the court goes on to rely on the reasoning in *Isaacs*, which points out the "fatal flaw" in relying solely on the rule to test foreseeability. The tension between the *Isaacs* view and the prior similars rule lead the court to express an approach to the overall assessment of foreseeability, which is the basis of the method that is outlined here as the most reasonable.

Evidence of prior similar incidents is not the *sine qua non* to a finding of foreseeability... While proof of prior similar incidents is probative of foreseeability, such proof is not the prerequisite, and its absence does not foreclose a finding of foreseeability.[25]

Conclusion

While there are still jurisdictions that rely exclusively on a strict application of the prior similars rule in some cases, the overall force of the rule is on the decline. This is not to say that the attention to prior similar incidents as a factor in determining foreseeability is necessarily lessening, but the trend seems to be toward broader "reasonableness" tests such as those in *Isaacs* and *Kline*, which allow consideration of more factors.

In the face of this, it is necessary for litigants and landowners to possess a clear understanding of both a definition of reasonable foreseeability that is consistent with the vague guidelines set out by the legal tests, and also a concrete method for assessing whether crime is in fact reasonably foreseeable in a given situation.

The development of these concepts will be the focus of the next section of this book.

Endnotes

1. *Kline v. 1500 Massachusetts Avenue Apartment Corporation*, 439 F.2d 477 (D.C. Cir. 1970), 483, quoting *Goldberg v. Housing Authority of Newark*, 186 A.2d 291, (N.J. 1962).
2. *Kline, supra*, 483.
3. *Ibid.*, 481.
4. *Ibid.*
5. *Ibid.*, 483.
6. *Isaacs v. Huntington Memorial Hospital*, 38 Cal.3d 112, 695 P.2d 653, 211 Cal.Rptr. 356 (1985), 360, quoting *Taylor v. Centennial Bowl, Inc.*, 65 Cal.2d 114, 121 (1966).
7. *Rowland v. Christian*, 443 P.2d 561, 70 Cal.Rptr. 97 (1968).
8. *Isaacs, supra*, 360-361, quoting Rest.2d Torts, section 344, comment (f).

9. *Gomez v. Ticor*, 145 Cal.App.3d 622, 193 Cal.Rptr. 600, 605 (1983).

10. *Ibid.*

11. *Webster's Ninth New Collegiate Dictionary. s. v.* "foresee."

12. *Gomez, supra*, 604, quoting *Bigbee v. Pacific Telephone & Telegraph Co.* (1983), 192 Cal.Rptr. 857, quoting 2 Harper & James, *Law of Torts* (1956) Section 18.2, 1020.

13. *Loeser v. Nathan Hale Gardens, Inc.*, 73 A.D.2d 187, 425 N.Y.S.2d 104, (1980), 109.

14. *Wingard v. Safeway Stores, Inc.*, 123 Cal.App.3d 37, 176 Cal.Rptr. 320 (1981), 43.

15. *Moody v. Cawdrey & Associates*, 721 P.2d 708 (Haw. 1986), p. 712, note 8.

16. *Ibid.*, quoting *Scott v. Watson*, 359 A.2d 548 (1976), 554.

17. *Walkoviak v. Hilton Hotels Corp.*, 580 S.W.2d 623 (Tex. 1979)

18. *C.S. v. Sophir*, 368 N.W.2d 447 (Neb. 1985)

19. *Ibid., supra*, 446.

20. *Kwaitkowski v. Superior Trading Co.*, 123 Cal.App.3d 324, 176 Cal.Rptr. 494 (1981), 497.

21. *Ibid.*

22. *Isaacs, supra*, 361.

23. *Isaacs, supra*, 362, quoting *Weirum v. RKO General, Inc.*, 123 Cal.Rptr. 468 (1975), 47.

24. *Moody, supra*, 712.

25. *Ibid.*, 715.

CRIME FORESEEABILITY

CHAPTER FOUR

A Model of Foreseeability

As evidenced in previous case summaries, the concept of foreseeability has been the subject of interpretation by various courts across the country. Part of the confusion lies in a lack of understanding of the criteria required to develop the data necessary to determine crime foreseeability.

Aside from the legal reasoning, a practical aspect must be applied to provide reasonableness and logic to any finding of crime foreseeability. Without established criteria, anyone can predict or guess whether criminal assault can be anticipated without any sound basis for that opinion.

Foreseeability is a Statistical Concept

For the purposes of this type of litigation, crime foreseeability can be described as a statistical concept. A statistical concept, in the broad sense used here, is an evaluation of potential, which relies on experience and interprets it using both quantitative and qualitative methods. Such an evaluation need not be based solely on numerical data and calculations, but it must employ a balancing process that weighs all relevant data in a prescribed manner.

The purpose of this model is to present a framework in which relevant data can be recognized and assigned weight in a final evaluation. The emphasis is not on presenting a complete discussion of foreseeability in every situation but on developing a cohesive methodology, which, intelligently applied, will result in a sound assessment of whether crime in a particular situation is reasonably foreseeable.

First, a brief discussion of what is meant by quantitative and qualitative methods of evaluation in this context is in order.

Quantitative Analysis

Quantitative evaluation involves the analysis of numerical data (empirical) describing the crime history of a site and often the surrounding area. While extremely valuable in assessing high rates of foreseeability, this type of analysis can comment only on incidents that have been reported in the past.

As recognized by the courts in *Isaacs*, *Moody*, and *Kwaitkowski*, this method can be insensitive to considerations such as changes in the use of a facility, new management, new construction, and rapid changes in the character of neighborhoods; it thus may not provide a completely reliable picture of the foreseeability of crime.

Quantitative analysis also involves a decision making process for processing crime statistics. Criteria are established that limit the type of crimes to be evaluated, as well as the geographic area, class of assailants, and timeframes.

A widely read paper, which has been put forth as a standard, states flatly that the proper method for assessing foreseeability is to research all stranger-to-stranger crimes, within a one mile radius of the crime site, within the last two years.

As attractive as such a method is for its simplicity, crime foreseeability cannot always be evaluated by uniform time and distance criteria. In an urban area, a one mile radius would generally be too broad, losing the relevant data among useless statistics. One mile could extend past the boundaries of a city, county, or police reporting zone, resulting in invalid data comparisons.

Crimes committed eight blocks away from a site are of little use in relation to many premises, especially if major physical or psychological barriers exist, such as a freeway or railroad tracks between the two areas.

Time periods suffer from the same decay factors. Neighborhoods and conditions can change drastically in less than a year. By the same token, static neighborhoods may reflect little change for five years or more.

There is a danger inherent in the arbitrary determination of flexible parameters, and this is a problem to which untempered quantitative analysis is especially vulnerable.

Qualitative Analysis

Qualitative evaluation essentially includes lifelong experience of land occupants, instinct, intuition, and physical observations of similar environments, which provide the basis for the ordinary estimates of a location's safety.

Among the considerations here are the physical attributes of a property and the reputation of the property and its surrounding area. Cold statistics cannot provide this information.

Qualitative analysis is best conducted in person by a skilled security practitioner, who will survey the site and neighborhood and interview area inhabitants. This type of survey often provides clues to the type and amount of unreported crime and the level of fear regarding crime, as well as noting physical conditions at a site and surrounding areas.

This type of evaluation best lends itself to the examination of a site from a criminal's point of view and enables one to realistically analyze the potential effects of various attributes of the site on the future behavior of criminals in the absence of a history of crime.

Crime Foreseeability Evaluation Components

There are three easily distinguishable components of a premises, called *factors* here, to consider when assessing crime foreseeability. Certain elements exist within these factors that may or may not contribute to foreseeable crime.

The three component factors are (1) nature of the premises, (2) crime demographics, and (3) location.

If investigation of any one of these factors points to foreseeable crime, then it is impossible to escape the issue of foreseeability. However, to determine the level and type of crime foreseeability, all three factors must be considered.

For example, assume that a popular nightclub catering to young people has a rear parking lot, where prior assaults have occurred. The nature of the premises is one that will have alcohol, loud music, and young people looking for a good time jammed into a small space; the location of the parking lot in the rear reduces supervision; and the crime history speaks for itself as being potentially dangerous. The elements associated with these three factors in this case serve to enhance rather than to diminish assaultive crime potential. In this example, it is probable that assaultive crime is foreseeable, and further investigation is thus warranted.

Conditions

Affecting the elements of the three factors are various *conditions*. Examples of conditions could be lighting, frequency of security patrols, an unlocked door, or a large hole in a fence. A condition may only aggravate or mitigate the tendency of a factor element to increase or decrease crime foreseeability.

These conditions cannot in themselves prove or preclude crime foreseeability, but only serve to affect the overall impact of a given element on the level of foreseeability.

For example, overgrown shrubbery on the ground level is a condition that would not normally affect the foreseeability of a sexual assault inside of a third floor apartment unit.

Litigants on both sides of a dispute frequently overestimate the potential persuasive force of their crime foreseeability arguments by allowing the entire case to hinge on one or more of these conditions without pursuing the complete analysis presented here.

The most effective approach to assessing foreseeability is to consider the three factors in order. Consider the nature of the premises, crime demographics, and lastly location.

What follows is a brief discussion regarding each of the three component factors in the order in which they should be considered and an examination of a few of the main elements associated with them.

A more complete discussion of each component factor, its associated elements, and its conditions will follow in subsequent chapters.

Nature of Premises

It is essential to the evaluation of crime demographics to first have a complete understanding of the elements associated with the nature of the premises.

The premises type and usage will impact the probative value of different crime classifications to be considered during the analysis. For example, property crimes inside a shopping mall are often excluded when evaluating the foreseeability of an abduction and rape in the parking structure.

The major elements involved in the nature of the premises factor are whether the premises is a business or a residence, the hours of operation, the extent that the premises are open to public, type of clientele, and type of service or product available. A business that remains open to the public twenty-four hours a day will have foreseeable crime types different from a limited-hour operation that is semiprivate.

For example, an apartment complex in a retirement community should usually anticipate fewer assaults than a apartment complex near a college campus simply due to the nature of its tenants and guests. Bars and nightclubs that provide alcoholic beverages and live entertainment and that cater to younger crowds can be expected to have more crime problems than a more subdued establishment and older age group.

A judge went on the record to flatly state that in his opinion convenience stores and urban parking lots, by their very nature, provide a special temptation to crime.[1]

Following that logic, it seems reasonable to predict that certain types of crimes are foreseeable simply by the mere nature of a premises. For example, shopping malls and parking lots should expect auto related crimes (e.g., auto burglary, vandalism, auto theft). Whether this criminal activity on site escalates to personal assaults is another issue.

A twenty-four hour convenience store with a single clerk on duty should anticipate that robbery is foreseeable. Various conditions, discussed later, will help determine what level of foreseeability actually exists for robbery and other violent crimes.

Crime Demographics

Elements involved in evaluating previous crime are a determination of which crime classifications are relevant, the relevant radius around the incident, the proper time frame, the type and precision of data available, and an estimate of the proportion of crimes that are officially documented.

The consideration of above criteria into an analysis is called *crime demographics*. It is a complete breakdown of statistics that is more precise and informative than raw numbers.

In certain cases where the other two factors, nature and location of premises, do not produce strong and compelling indicators, the absence of significant and relevant crime demographics can eliminate the possibility of a finding of crime foreseeability.

Location

The location of the premises is the *factor* that in itself would give rise to the *least* substantial determination of crime foreseeability of the three. Also, its relative importance is generally subject to what has been found through investigation of the other two factors, and it is the most likely to be influenced by conditions.

The major elements within this factor are general location in the city, relationship to other businesses and residences, population density, economic demographics of the relevant area, and proximity to major traffic arteries. More specific elements include whether the incident location is on the ground floor or an upper floor, in a public common area or semiprivate area.

The concept of location as a major factor causes us to focus on the "where" issue in crime foreseeability. All crime types are not foreseeable everywhere. A rapist who gained access through a fourth floor exterior window of a high-rise apartment by using mountain climbing gear and superior skill would not be reasonably anticipated and therefore not normally foreseeable.

However, a recently constructed 24-hour convenience store in the center of the highest crime zone in the city should anticipate a variety of property and personal crimes because of its location alone. Its level of crime foreseeability should be considered as potentially moderate to high from opening day. Its actual level and type of crime foreseeability will be modified later and affected by the actual nature of the business and its ability to control criminal activity through use of security techniques.

Types of Conditions

Conditions can be broken down into two main categories, physical conditions and procedures. Physical conditions would include lighting, noise, hardware (e.g., fences, locks, alarms, video cameras), foliage, signage, visibility, and pedestrian and vehicle traffic flow. Procedural conditions would include cash handling policies, a schedule for locking certain doors and turning on lights, a key control system, and security guard patrol methods, as well as procedures for reporting incidents and repairing any problems.

Mere conditions, even if present in great numbers, *cannot* be used to determine crime foreseeability alone. Even though certain conditions may seem to have had much to do with the actual commission of a crime, this in itself does not address the issue of crime foreseeability. To avoid this problem, conditions should be considered not merely for their role in a particular crime, but for those attributes that affect crime foreseeability.

For example, lighting may be on or off, brightly illuminated or dim, located effectively or not; door locking hardware may be locked or unlocked; and guard patrols may be scheduled only for six hour shifts on weekends.

Frequently in premises liability cases, a plaintiff will allege that the proximate cause of a client's assault and injuries was poor lighting or a lack of uniformed security patrol in a parking lot. Both lighting and frequency of security patrol issues are mere conditions, yet cases have been won and lost based solely on these issues. Surely there are thousands of parking lots, with similar lighting and no security patrols, which have operated safely for many years. Therefore, the existence of poor lighting and guard patrols alone cannot indicate that assaultive crime was foreseeable just because a single incident occurred.

However, when one applies the above issues to a parking lot in a high crime location, whose adjacent business nature attracts young people to a site where crime demographics show a history of personal assaults involving young people, then conditions of inadequate lighting and infrequent security patrols aggravate the above factors and become relevant in supporting an allegation of inadequate security.

Determining Levels of Crime Foreseeability

Merely to say that crime is foreseeable on a particular premises is not enough. For property owners and business operators to function within the scope of their legal duty to protect their land entrants, they must know what crimes types are reasonably foreseeable, at what expected frequency, and what steps can be taken that will later be deemed adequate should a criminal incident occur.

Actual crime demographics can be expected to differ in frequency and crime type for each premises and location within a premises; it is therefore necessary to analyze the statistics to distinguish between them. The results of this analysis should enable a security expert to determine a relative level of crime foreseeability for each property surveyed. The analysis should further identify what crime types are more foreseeable than others and in what specific locations within the premises is crime likely to occur.

Levels of Crime Foreseeability

The analysis of the three crime foreseeability factors should generate an opinion that will assign the potential for crime into one of four levels.

Crime potential is either (1) not foreseeable, (2) low, (3) moderate, or (4) high.

These levels of foreseeability must have elastic values to allow the business community and/or trier of fact (judge or jury) to have a range in which to categorize their understanding of the information at hand. It is conceivable that a particular crime type could fall on the borderline between low and moderate or moderate and high.

The level of "not foreseeable," however, is not as flexible, by design. If a particular crime on a property is believed to be not foreseeable by the court, to the extent that it finds that no reasonable jury could find otherwise, then the issue becomes a matter of law, not fact, and can be dismissed by the court in response to a motion for summary judgment.

The three remaining levels of foreseeability are designed to identify that amount of security that is required for premises owners or operators to meet and discharge their legal duty of care.

Precise values for each level are not used because of variables such as accuracy of data, uniqueness of the premises, and the fact that criminals cannot be counted on to act in a consistent manner. However, the assessment of risk and vulnerability has always been established by human experience.

Security experts experienced with litigation case preparation have an advantage of having a basis of comparison from performing many previous security surveys and crime demographic studies. Some experts will have libraries of previous studies and local crime statistics to aid in their comparison and analysis.

A respected author on risk analysis wrote:

> Several well-known authorities have concluded that order of magnitude expressions such as low, moderate and high to indicate relative degrees of risk are more than adequate for most risk control surveys.
>
> The use of the terms low, moderate and high equate roughly with probability ranges (on a scale of 1 to 10) of 1-3, 4-6, and 7-10, respectively.[2]

Another well-known national security consulting firm utilizes a powerful computer to analyze U. S. crime/census data and other public records and scores a site survey questionnaire completed by the premises operator.

The information is developed into a crime index that, it is claimed, can predict the crimes against persons (CAP) vulnerability at a given site relative to the predicted average criminal vulnerability of its environment.

This crime index number is then plotted on a graph and compared against a three level range labeled as "L" "M" and "H" respectively. The authors of this program define the middle graph point as "M," denoting a predicted vulnerability equal to that of its environment. The upper graph point "H" indicates a predicted vulnerability five times greater than the local average, and the lower graph point

"L" denotes a predicted vulnerability five times less than the environment average.[3]

These consultants and others realize that three separate levels of crime foreseeability are necessary to allow premises operators to gauge their security effectiveness relative to that of the outside environment and against commonly used security practices or industry guidelines.

What has been missing historically from these evaluations is the impact of existing security measures on the external crime demographics.

For example, a crime demographics survey of an apartment complex may indicate a moderate to high assaultive crime rate in the surrounding area. However, due to superior security measures in place, the actual crime history of the premises may be quite low by comparison.

What level of crime foreseeability does one assign? What level of security is required to meet the legal duty imposed by each level of foreseeability? These questions and more will answered in the discussion that follows.

Not Foreseeable

A finding of not foreseeable is a legal decision made by the court and not by a jury. However, attorneys must first submit declarations (arguments) in suppoert of their motions to the court for consideration of a ruling. Historically, the reasons stated for crimes ruled to be not foreseeable are: (1) absence of prior similar crimes, (2) lack of knowledge or notice to the land owner, (3) the crime was too bizarre to protect against, (4) and others.

Probably the most well known recent case where a crime was ruled to be not foreseeable was in the case of the mass murder at McDonald's restaurant in Southern California.[4] A gunman, armed with assault rifles, suddenly appeared on the property and starting shooting at random, killing or wounding 32 victims without provocation. The court stated that the defendant restaurant had *no* duty to take steps to prevent an event that was inherently unforeseeable.

Low Crime Foreseeability

Low crime foreseeability is defined as a level such that after considering the nature, location, and crime demographics, a reasonable and thoughtful person would not anticipate assaultive crime while on the premises. This opinion would be supported by the absence of previous assaultive crimes during the past two or three years; and crimes preceding that period would be too statistically remote in time.

Whole regions in a city can be considered low crime areas due primarily to their socioeconomic makeup and zoning. Moderate and high crime regions can have pockets of low crime areas, and even individual businesses can obtain a low crime foreseeability level by operating with effective security controls in place.

As discussed earlier, certain premises could be assigned the level of low foreseeability prior to being open just by the nature and sometimes the location of the property.

A low crime foreseeability level has an upward limit that will be tested as assaultive crime occurs. If the quantitative and qualitative data still support a low probability of crime reoccurring, then current levels of security could still be deemed adequate. This data should be supported by an absence of fear of crime by the premises inhabitants and the presence of feelings of control over their environment. Most premises in the United States fall into the low crime foreseeability level, with the possible exception of certain sections of some urban cities and resort areas.

Moderate Crime Foreseeability

Moderate crime foreseeability is defined as a level such that after considering the nature, location, and crime demographics, a reasonable and thoughtful person would anticipate the possibility of assaultive crime while on the premises.

This opinion should be supported by crime demographics on the site and surrounding area that indicate only a limited number of previous assaultive crimes over the past several years but that do not fit any identifiable pattern or trend. The number of assaultive crimes is still too statistically uninformative to warrant any single radical response to prevent future occurrence. However, a moderate level of crime foreseeability should have originally generated a combination of security precautions to prevent future crimes of a similar nature or at a similar location from reoccurring.

A moderate level of crime foreseeability should be evidenced by an average amount of awareness and fear of crime while on the premises. The reasonable person will take advantage of available security measures and will use common sense to limit exposure to potential danger. For example, apartment and hotel tenants will keep windows secured and use available door locks, dead bolts, peepholes, and security chains. They will walk in well lighted, populated areas or wait for an appropriate escort.

It is possible for a premises to implement effective security precautions that will reduce exposure to the level of low crime foreseeability. Many urban premises are at this moderate level, and operators attempt to maintain security precautions to reduce crime to its lowest possible level.

Unfortunately, the success of a sound security plan can backfire if one decides to cut back on security expense or fails to maintain the existing level of security precautions believing the problem to be solved. When this occurs, patrons and tenants sometimes become angered by the cutback in security and apparent disregard for their personal safety. In my experience, these victims make up a large class of premises liability litigants.

High Crime Foreseeability

High crime foreseeability is defined as a level such that after considering the nature, location, and crime demographics, a reasonable person would actually anticipate that an assaultive crime may occur at any time.

This opinion would be supported by crime demographics that showed a pattern of assaultive and other crimes on the premises and in the surrounding area continuously for several years. The prior number of assaultive crimes would statistically suggest a high probability of continued assaults if radical security precautions are not implemented, or if the nature of the premises remains unmodified.

The physical premises usually shows signs of vandalism, burglary attempts, and general disrepair. The neighborhood exhibits physical security precautions such as bars on the windows, alarm boxes, and perimeter fences. Inhabitants experience an elevated fear of crime, together with a feeling of losing control over their environment.

The premises will typically have a bad reputation in the eyes of the surrounding neighbors and law enforcement personnel. The premises operator may feel that the costs of security precautions are not affordable and would have little effect on crime anyway.

A continuing level of high crime foreseeability is unacceptable in our society because it is against public policy to allow a dangerous condition to exist in premises accessed by the public for the benefit of the premises owner and operator.

A business or residence in a high crime area can implement radical security precautions to control its incidence of assaultive crime. If successful, it is possible to reduce exposure to a moderate crime foreseeability level. However, the outside threat will continue, waiting for a breakdown in security.

A premises owner may have no choice but to consider changing the nature of the business (e.g., from a twenty-four hour liquor store to a limited hour groceries only store) or relocating.

Variables in Crime Foreseeability

Often a premises liability litigation will focus on a specific location within a property and alleged inadequate security based on a design or mechanical defect in a security device. When this occurs, it becomes necessary to evaluate the crime foreseeability level for a specific factor such as a particular location, type of crime, or time of day.

It is possible to have two or more different levels of crime foreseeability on the same property. For example, a convenience store in a moderate crime location during the day can increase its crime foreseeability level to high between the hours 10:00 pm and 2:00 am when all surrounding businesses are closed and traffic counts are reduced; ground floor apartments in a building can have a high burglary history compared to a very low crime experience on upper floors, due primarily to accessibility.

Additionally, it would be difficult for a property owner to reasonably foresee, for example: a rape inside a third floor apartment of a security building when adequate door and window locks were provided but not used; the possibility of a person firing an automatic weapon inside a convenience store at midday with several customers inside; or the accidental shooting of a customer in the parking lot of a shopping mall by rival gangs who do not frequent the area.

Any premises liability evaluation must be prepared to specify a level of crime foreseeability for the site, the surrounding area, and in particular locations within the property. In addition, the evaluation should draw attention to the crime types to be anticipated. Once this is achieved, an analysis of existing security measures can be made.

The question is *not* whether the crime at issue could have been prevented or not, but rather if the security precautions in place were adequate to prevent the type of crime that should have been reasonably anticipated.

Conclusion

An established criterion for determining a level of crime foreseeability must be utilized in order to provide a sound basis for opinion testimony. Otherwise, expert opinion testimony will be based on guesswork, uncertain predictions, and whim.

The criteria outlined here will allow for a complete analysis, which can be presented to a jury in an understandable fashion, and which should be viewed with a high degree of credibility.

The results of the analysis will identify a level of crime foreseeability, which can be used to evaluate the adequacy of an existing security program on a premises.

Endnotes

1. *Isaacs v. Huntington Memorial Hospital*, 38 Cal.3d 112, 695 P.2d 653, 211 Cal.Rptr. 356 (Cal. 1985), 364-5.
2. James F. Broder, *Risk Analysis and the Security Survey* (Boston: Butterworth Publishers, 1984), 32-33.
3. CAP Index Vulnerability Analysis. King of Prussia, PA.: CAP Index, Inc.
4. *Lopez v. McDonald's*, 193 Cal.App.3d 495, 238 Cal.Rptr. 436 (1987)

CHAPTER FIVE

Nature of the Premises

The first of the three factors to be considered when evaluating crime foreseeability is the nature of the premises. The mere nature of the premises alone will often indicate that crime is foreseeable, the types of crimes that can be anticipated, and the types of security precautions that are commonly used in the industry to combat those crimes.

In order to develop a clear understanding of what elements and conditions exist in various premises, we will review examples of five different property types. The different property types will have elements unique unto themselves, as well as elements in common with other properties.

The selected property types are: convenience stores, shopping centers, apartment complexes, hotels/motels, and parking lots.

Apartment complexes and hotels/motels will be used to illustrate the type of crimes commonly associated with residential properties, while convenience stores and shopping centers will be used to illustrate the type of crimes commonly associated with commercial/retail stores. Residential properties are usually considered as semi-private, for tenants and guests only, while retail stores are usually considered public. Parking lots have a common link between the other four types of premises but will be affected by crime types differently, depending on the premises served.

The following five scenarios are examples of poorly secured properties to illustrate how conditions and other factors can change the nature of a premises. It is important to understand that all of these premises types have the potential of operating safely. A well-run facility may not be affected by the same conditions or exposure to assaultive crime as in these examples.

When considering the elements and conditions of each property, try to imagine what crime types might be reasonably anticipated by considering the nature of the premises alone. Also consider what age, sex, or class of people might be involved in the criminal activity, and what time of day is most likely to be targeted.

Convenience Stores

What is the nature of a 24-hour convenience store as it relates to assaultive crime foreseeability? To answer this question, one must examine what elements and conditions are present, and how other factors affect it.

Our hypothetical convenience store has the following elements: it is open 24 hours per day and 365 days per year; it is a small store of 2400 square feet; it sells fast foods, beer/wine, cigarettes, and some groceries; the clientele consists mainly of neighborhood blue collar workers and high school students during the day and primarily young adult males after dark; it is a cash business; it has easy access to a major thoroughfare; and the store has high traffic counts until 10:00 pm on weekdays and until 2:00 am on weekends.

This store is affected by the following conditions: the store has good nighttime lighting inside the store, but poor illumination in the parking lot; the flood light in the rear of the building has been vandalized; the rear perimeter fence has a large hole and is used as a short cut to an adjacent housing project; graffiti and heavy litter are evident on the sides and rear of the store; two employees are on duty at night; a lone female employee is afraid to control loitering in the parking lot and in the rear of the building during the day; the store has poor cash handling procedures and does not use a drop safe; the store owner cashes welfare and social security checks twice a month; the store has a phony video surveillance camera and uses mirrors to watch the aisles; there are three public telephones attached to the exterior of the building, which are used heavily by the housing project tenants; on weekends and after sporting events, a third employee is added at night to help with additional sales and to watch inside the store for shoplifters; and the police drive through the parking lot approximately five times every night.

This convenience store will further be affected by the other two factors, location and crime demographics. It is located on a corner in a lower economic class residential neighborhood, consisting of rental apartments and subsidized housing; no other businesses are in the area; and a high school is located three blocks away. The crime history for the surrounding area is high for property crimes and moderate for crimes against persons.

Assuming the hypothetical factors, elements and conditions listed above, what types of assaultive crimes are reasonably foreseeable just by the nature of the premises alone? Robbery of the store or patrons, assault in the parking lot, purse snatch, and assault with deadly weapon are all probable if no crime prevention measures are in existence.

Because the store is an all night operation, these crimes have a higher potential of being committed after peak hours, when fewer witnesses are present. Intoxicated patrons tend to be more prevalent between 1:30 am and 2:30 am when the bars close and when they are looking for something else to eat or drink. Arguments over liquor sales after hours are to be expected, with some escalating to assault and battery.

The mere nature of this particular convenience store has the potential to bring together a volatile mix of patrons: students after sporting events, drunks trying to beat the 2:00 am liquor sales curfew, undesirables loitering, and foot traffic from the housing project. Certain conditions such as the vandalized flood light on the rear of the building, the hole in the fence, and evidence of past loitering will tend to aggravate the elements involved in the nature of this convenience store and support an increased probability of assaultive crime foreseeability.

The nature of this store would lend itself to support a crime history of five robberies in two years and previously assaulted employees and customers. Continued daily verbal abuse from undesirable loiterers, and daily theft of beer and wine by young adults who flee through the hole in the fence to the housing project would also be expected.

Because of the nature of this convenience store and its clientele, strict security measures need to be added to control any potentially harmful interaction between customers and neighborhood groups.

This store owner could attempt to reduce the level of assaultive crime foreseeability by changing the nature of present business practices and implement a security maintenance procedure. For example: the rear fence could be repaired; the outside lighting could be enhanced; the anti-loitering policy could be enforced, and litter and graffiti removed.

The addition of a robbery prevention training program including cash handling techniques and functional security devices, plus elimination of the excess cash required to cash welfare and social security checks, should significantly reduce the likelihood of assaultive crimes on the premises. The implementation of the above changes should assist in attracting a more mature, stable clientele back into the store who had been previously frightened away.

Shopping Centers

The nature of a shopping center as it relates to assaultive crime foreseeability is determined by first examining what elements and conditions are present and how other factors may affect it.

Our hypothetical shopping center has the following elements: it is a large regional shopping center of approximately one million square feet; it leases retail space to six major department stores and over a hundred smaller retail shops; the mall is fully enclosed; it is open to the public 365 days per year from 9:00 am until 9:00 pm; there are attached movie theaters; restaurants and bars have private exterior access and remain open after midnight; the shopping center draws patrons from several miles away; customers spend several hours on the premises; cash, checks, and credit cards are used; the shopping center has a three-tiered, split-level design; the parking structure has five stories and is fully enclosed; lone female customers often walk through the parking structure with purchases; the parking structure is only accessible by vehicle, and traffic counts are high; public transportation directly services the shopping center; great numbers of customers and employees consisting of a cross section of age groups, sexes, and races; teenagers tend to hang out during afternoons and weekends; and customer counts are very high on weekends and during the Christmas holiday season.

This shopping center is affected by the following conditions: visibility inside the shopping center is severely restricted because of the split-level design; interior response times by in-house security and police are slow because of having to use public escalators and elevators; the parking structure has minimum illumination and is noisy; portable radio transmission by the security guards is affected when inside the parking structure; video cameras are installed on every floor of the parking structure but not in operation yet; one mobile uniformed security guard per shift is assigned to patrol the entire parking structure; by tenant policy, all employees who work in the shopping center must park their vehicles on the fifth floor of the parking structure; and employee vehicles have parking stickers affixed to their right rear bumper for identification.

Foreseeable assaultive crimes associated with the above hypothetical nature of this shopping center would include parking lot assault, purse snatch, robbery, and possibly kidnap or rape. The extent that the conditions listed above aggravate control of the parking lot will determine the frequency of the foreseeable crimes.

The infrequent security guard patrol, vehicle noise, poor visibility, inoperative video cameras, and radio communication problems may offer little protection or deterrent value. The effect of the shopping center interior design may benefit the criminal by providing the necessary concealment and escape potential.

The density and number of potential targets makes a shopping center ideal for certain criminals. Criminals confronted in the middle of committing a property crime, such as an auto burglary, have occasionally become violent and have injured the person attempting to stop them.

Location of the shopping center will have little impact on crime foreseeability unless adjacent residential areas or schools provide a significant amount of foot traffic, or the shopping center itself is surrounded by a high crime area.

Crime history of the surrounding area does not always affect the nature of a shopping center because of its ability to attract large groups of patrons from outside the immediate area. Due to this fact, shopping centers will often develop a crime history that is comparable only with itself.

Peak hours for crime are usually business hours, and crime consists largely of fraud, petty and grand theft, and auto related crimes. Crimes against persons are usually committed in the parking lots and other isolated areas and vary by time of day. Enclosed parking structures are not affected by darkness and shadows as would be open lots, due to interior lighting.

The nature of this shopping center will be dictated more by the clientele who frequent the premises, due to the impact of the facility design and the range of its customer base.

Because of these design problems, the frequency of assaultive crimes will be directly correlated to the number, deployment, and effectiveness of security personnel and law enforcement officers.

Shopping centers can gain a reputation for being dangerous by allowing gangs of undesirables to loiter. This reputation over time will drive away a mature, stable, law abiding clientele, leaving the undesirables as the customer base.

Hotels and Motels

The nature a hotel or motel, as it relates to crime foreseeability, is determined by first examining what elements and conditions are present and how other factors may affect them.

Our hypothetical hotel/motel has the following elements: it consists of one large building and is three-stories high; it caters to travelers off a major interstate highway; it is considered to be a budget lodging facility; there are 110 rental units and each unit is accessed from an exterior common walkway; each unit has a solid door, deadbolt lock, security chain, peephole, and a direct dial telephone; the building has three outside stairways accessing the upper floors; the rear of the building faces a vacant lot; the registration office faces the street with the rental units directly behind it in a row; the only driveway into the property passes the registration office but also services an adjacent restaurant; the parking lot allows immediate access to lower floor units; an on-site management is available 24-hours; a separately owned 24-hour restaurant and bar is immediately adjacent and shares the same piece of land.

This hotel/motel is affected by the following conditions: ninety percent of guest turnover is daily; no key control system exists; maintenance of window and door security hardware is excellent; guest's occasionally forget to turn in their keys upon checkout; lighting is excellent in the parking lot but almost nonexistent on the back of the building facing the vacant lot; patrons from the adjacent bar often park in the motel parking lot; prostitutes who frequent the bar sometimes uses the motel for their clients; foot traffic is limited to hotel/motel guests and restaurant and bar patrons; law enforcement does not patrol on the property nor is there any security patrol; the land owner lives out of state and is not interested in improving the property; the motel owner lives on-site; the restaurant owner has been unwilling to address the hotel/motel owner's complaints about after hour problems in his parking lot.

The two other factors, location and crime demographics, affect this hotel/motel in the following ways: it is located at the far end of a resort town off a four-lane thoroughfare and visible from a major highway, and the property is somewhat isolated other than the adjacent restaurant. Crime demographic research shows that auto related crimes and parking lot vandalism is high; room burglaries are low; crimes against persons such as robbery, assault, and rape are moderate but have been isolated to the prostitute clientele, restaurant and bar patrons, and to hotel guests known to each other. Crime in the surrounding area is almost nonexistent due to the location of the motel outside of town.

Foreseeable assaultive crimes associated with this hypothetical hotel/motel could include parking lot crimes such as assault, purse snatch, robbery, and sex crimes. Because of the absence of a key control system, inside room assaults are foreseeable regardless of a lack of prior reported incidents. Because the property is located off a major highway and caters to travelers, local crime patterns are difficult to predict. However, this same isolation often means far less typical crime when compared to its urban counterpart.

In this case even though the motel property and security hardware are maintained, the adjacent restaurant and bar patrons are spilling over onto the motel property and creating the potential for injury to a guest. One solution would be to build a fence between the two businesses, but would should pay? Another solution might be to hire a security guard to patrol after dark. However, due to the proximity of the two properties, how would the security guard know which persons were motel guests, which were restaurant patrons, and which were trespassers? In addition, each property owner has different requirements and policies. For example, the restaurant will not want a security guard to harass paying customers, while the motel owner will not want a guard lurking directly outside of sleeping room windows or conversing with prostitutes.

This is a classic scenario where there are multiple property owners and neither want to bear the costs of providing security measures. Obviously, a three-way split would seem a logical solution. However, in this situation only one party, the restaurant, is the major cause of the danger. This conflict of property design, ownership, and responsibility for action are the basis for numerous lawsuits alleging inadequate security and crime foreseeability. Because of this arrangement all three property owners are likely to be named as co-defendants in a premises liability lawsuit involving a parking lot assault.

Apartment Complexes

The nature of an apartment complex, as it relates to crime foreseeability, is determined by first examining what elements and conditions are present and how other factors may affect them.

Our hypothetical apartment complex has the following elements: it consists of six freestanding buildings; each building is four stories high; each building contains 100 rental units; each apartment is accessed from a common hallway; each building has a main common entry door and elevator lobby; each building has two side fire stairways and exit doors; each building has an intercom/telephone access control system at the main entry doors; each building main door is self-closing and locking; the ground floor units can also be accessed through individual unit sliding glass doors; parking is available in a lighted, subterranean garage with assigned spaces; access to the apartment complex property is from two side streets and one major thoroughfare; and the tenant population is approximately 900 young adults.

This apartment complex is affected by the following conditions: tenant population turns over once every nine months; building entry and fire stairway doors are often propped open; no key control system exists; there is a heavy growth of bushes around the entrances to the buildings and parking garage; inconsistent illumination on the exterior walkways causes many dark shadows; the intercom/telephone system is often inoperable; student parties often attract undesirable non-tenants into the buildings; two security guards patrol the parking garage and building perimeters on foot from 6:00 pm until 6:00 am; and the local police patrol the perimeter driveways twice per shift.

The two other factors affect the apartment complex in the following ways: a state university is located two blocks away; a major bus route stops in front of the apartment complex; a four lane thoroughfare passes directly in front of the complex and links up with the freeway within one mile; and crime demographics research shows that auto, first floor burglary, and property crimes have a high foreseeability level, and crimes against persons, with concentrations in the parking lot and near building access points, have a moderate level of foreseeability.

Foreseeable assaultive crime, based on the factors and conditions associated with this hypothetical apartment complex, could include parking lot crime, assault, purse snatch, robbery, burglary, and sex crimes.

The ability of the apartment complex management to control and maintain the existing security hardware and procedures will be reflected in the crime demographics research. Security precautions such as controlling access to the buildings, increased visibility at night for the parking garage and access points for each building, and a tenant escort system would impact the majority of the stranger-to-stranger assaultive type crimes while on the premises. The use of an adequate number of personnel to maintain and monitor the security hardware and procedures would also be required.

Parking Lots

To determine whether crime is foreseeable due to the very nature of a parking lot, one must determine what elements and conditions are present and how other factors affect it.

Our hypothetical parking lot has the following elements: it is attached to a large discount department store and small shopping plaza consisting of a bank and five small retail shops; parking is free and open to the public 12 hours per day and 364 days per year while open for business; the discount department store caters to lower economic class families, and it does mainly a cash business; the large parking lot has high traffic counts at night and on weekends and is often full; and store employees must park together near the perimeter of the lot.

This parking lot is affected by the following conditions: nighttime illumination in the parking lot is at minimum near the store front and below minimum at the center and perimeter; women and children frequently carry purchases to their car; the in-store security staff or the police rarely patrol the parking lot; and high vehicle and foot traffic in the parking lot make it difficult to determine ownership of individual cars.

This parking lot will further be affected by the other two factors: it is located in a lower economic class neighborhood and adjacent to a freeway; there is a moderate to high property crime rate on the premises and in the surrounding area; and there is a moderate level of crimes against persons especially after 6:00 pm. The parking lot has a reputation for auto vandalism, stolen autos, and stereo theft.

Assuming the hypothetical factors, elements, and conditions outlined above, what types of assaultive crimes should be reasonably anticipated? Robbery, aggravated assault, purse snatch, kidnapping, and rape are all probable, along with a variety of auto related property crimes.

Parking lots, because of being open and isolated, limits the use of many security applications.

The use of security personnel to patrol in motorized vehicles with communication ability is about the only practical and effective solution for an open parking lot. High visibility, reporting ability, and quick response times by an adequate number of security guards will generally prevent or deter parking lot crimes. Improvement in the level of illumination will further enhance their visibility and provide a greater deterrent value.

Limiting perimeter parking lot ingress/egress points so that vehicles must pass in front of the stores will reduce the number and attractiveness of possible vehicle escape routes.

Procedures for nighttime employee escort and customer bag carryout services would be viable alternatives to consider in an effort to reduce exposure to personal assaults in certain parking lots.

Conclusion

The very nature of a premises and the conditions and other factors affecting it will often indicate what assaultive crimes should be reasonably anticipated. We should learn, by example, how other similar premises have been affected, and what particular security precautions were effective in controlling criminal assault.

Each premises owner or operator has some control over the elements that make up the nature of each business. Often, changes in the way a business operates will effectively reduce exposure to assaultive crime. Sometimes these operational changes are the only viable alternative to reducing exposure to assaultive crime and could even include closing down a business.

CHAPTER SIX

Crime Demographics

The second of the three *factors* to be considered when evaluating crime foreseeability is the crime demographics for the site and surrounding area. The crime history of a premises alone may indicate that certain assaultive crimes are indeed foreseeable by the mere fact that they occurred previously and within a relevant time period. This initial finding will dictate the need for more investigation including an evaluation of how the two remaining factors, nature of the premises and location, affect the crime foreseeability level.

Information regarding crime demographics on a property or surrounding area can be either formal or informal. Crime records, for instance, may be generated by a computer, logged by hand in a ledger, or recalled by witnesses. Information regarding the precise location, time of day, age of suspect, and method of operation can be obtained from these sources and are the component parts of a crime demographic analysis. It is important to gather as much information as possible to provide for a more complete analysis.

Crime Record Research

The primary purposes of researching crime records are twofold: (1) establish the frequency and type of crimes that have occurred on the property; and (2) establish the frequency and type of crimes that have occurred in the surrounding area. The secondary purpose for crime history research is to determine the characteristics of the perpetrator, time of crime, day of the week, specific location on site, and method of crime.

Crime record research involves more than gathering prior crime statistics. It involves developing knowledge of the environment surrounding a property and making judgements regarding what relevant types of crime should be analyzed and for what distance away from a property. It involves interviews in the field with property inhabitants, employees, neighbors, and police beat officers. It is impossible to evaluate crime foreseeability or the effectiveness of on-site security programs without field research.

Crime Research Sources

What follows is a discussion of the available crime demographic research sources that should be utilized in a premises liability case. This summary should be of benefit to both plaintiff and defense attorneys, as well as security professionals and business operators.

Crime data used for premises liability matters are usually obtained from five primary sources: (1) Uniform Crime Reports (UCR)[1]; (2) National Crime Survey (NCS)[2];

(3) local law enforcement; (4) in-house security reports; and (5) field interviews.

Except for Uniform Crime Reports and National Crime Surveys, all other sources of records have a local jurisdictional time decay factor to consider because many police agencies annually purge their computer records and archive physical crime reports. Ideally, local crime records should be obtained within one year following an incident. The decay factor accelerates after that time making record research up to three years less productive.

Uniform Crime Reports

The Uniform Crime Reporting Program (UCR) has been managed by the FBI since 1930 in an effort to collect crime statistics in a consistent manner across the nation. Information compiled by UCR contributors is forwarded to the FBI either directly from the local law enforcement agency or through a state-level UCR program. Approximately 41 states have mandatory reporting requirements in an effort to develop accuracy and consistency in reporting.

Seven criminal offenses were initially chosen to serve as an index for gauging fluctuations in the overall volume and rate of crime. Known jointly as the Crime Index, these offenses include the violent crimes of murder (including non-negligent manslaughter), forcible rape, robbery, aggravated assault, and property crimes of burglary, larceny-theft, and motor vehicle theft. By congressional mandate, arson was added as the eighth index offense in 1979.

UCR crime statistics are collated by region, geographic division, state, and city. The number of incidents reported are divided into the area population and indexed as the crime rate per 100,000 population. Problems with these statistics arise due the fact that certain population rates must be estimated since the last census. Certain crime rates must also be estimated due to variations in crime classification methods and reporting procedures. Also, cities and towns with populations of less than 25,000 must extrapolate their numbers to come up with a comparative index rating.

Most individual states use similar criteria to develop a statewide and even countywide crime index. Although these statistics provide interesting trend comparisons, they offer little benefit in determining crime foreseeability for a neighborhood community or specific site. These statistics do not take into consideration the nature of a particular premises or the effectiveness of its crime prevention programs.

Many criminologists are critical of the UCR data, claiming that they are inaccurate for the reasons cited above, and because they fail to factor in the amount of unreported crimes. They also argue that the policy of focusing primarily on only eight select crimes does not give a true picture of the national crime problem. Nevertheless, UCR reports provide a useful statistic.

National Crime Survey

The National Crime Survey is a victimization survey created in the mid-1960's, which has been conducted annually since 1973. It is a system where a sampling of the population is surveyed at random to determine who has been victimized. The surveys are conducted either by telephone, by mail, or by in-person interview.

Victimization surveys have determined that only about half of all felonies have been reported to the police. The surveys also learn of victims who do not report crimes and of their sex, age, race, and income level. The NCS has often produced different crime trends than the UCR, and often in opposing directions for the same time periods surveyed. Much like the UCR, the NCS provides little benefit to help us evaluate crime foreseeability on a particular property.

Law Enforcement Records

Law enforcement crime records can provide a wealth of information. Quality and quantity of records will vary depending on the jurisdiction, technology, and policies on releasing information. Since the early 1980's, many progressive police departments have computerized their records. This means that in certain jurisdictions, computer printouts can be generated that will break down crime records by date, location, crime type, case number, and responding officers. It is sometimes possible to obtain crime records for a specific address, the entire block, beat, district, and division depending on one's needs. Certain types of crime can be isolated as well for the same given locations.

In most jurisdictions, however, a computer printout will only list records in date or crime order for a larger reporting area such as a police beat, census tract, or district. Records in this format must be hand sorted by someone knowledgeable in police codes and crime classifications.

Some agencies maintain records on microfiche that must be viewed and recorded by hand. Still others require hand searching of individual incident reports to obtain the records. Whatever the technology, records are usually accessible for a least one year following an incident, after which they become more difficult to obtain.

Although computer printouts are helpful for summary information, the actual crime reports are of greater benefit.

The actual reports will contain names, addresses, and other identifiers of witnesses, employees, responding police officers, and detailed information of each offense. The reporting party on the crime report is sometimes the business operator. This little bit of information can be critical later on when trying to prove or defend against the business operator having knowledge of previous criminal activity.

Most police agencies require a subpoena and fees before releasing records. It should be standard practice to immediately subpoena relevant crime reports for at least two years prior to the incident. Crime records going back more than two years may be beneficial but are usually difficult to obtain. Crime occurrences after the date of an incident are normally irrelevant and are rarely admissible.

Calls for Service

A little known source of police records is what is known as "calls for service." These records are obtained from the police dispatch computer files. Although these records are used for a different purpose, they can produce a useful statistic. Most modern police dispatch computer systems can sort their files electronically by address and retrieve a list of calls to a particular location for the past several years.

The advantages are that all calls are logged with the initial crime complaint, even though an incident report may never be filed. This is very common for bars, hotels, and apartment complexes. For example, an anonymous caller might report a fight or screaming, and by the time the police arrive, the disturbing parties have already fled.

The dispatch computer will create a record showing the time of the call, the initial complaint, the location of the disturbance, the name, address, and phone number of the complainant, the police unit dispatched, and any sub-sequent action taken. The disadvantage is in the accuracy of the information. Occasionally addresses and crime type are given incorrectly to the police dispatcher. Many lay people will report a petty theft as a robbery or a domestic dispute as an assault. A low number or absence of calls to a par-ticular location is strong evidence for the defense.

Try to obtain records for at least two years prior to the incident. As with all other records, these will eventually become unavailable depending upon each jurisdiction's purging timetable.

In-House Security Reports

The second major source for site specific crime records is the security reports, if any, written by on-site security personnel. Many large business operators have security personnel on-site. Security guard personnel who are employees of the business are called "proprietary" guards. Security services that are hired from an outside guard ser-vice are called a "contract" guard force. Both types of security guard staffs often complete daily activity and crime incident reports as well as other memoranda.

These reports are usually more informative than police crime reports because they describe the day-to-day ac-tivities of the premises. Many incidents that would be relevant to a litigating party are not reported to the police. On the other hand, many crime incidents are reported directly to the police and not to the security guards. For example, most people would call the police directly to report a purse snatch in a shopping center parking lot rather than report to mall security.

This information is only infrequently passed on to the business operator or security staff, unless they are somehow involved. The combination of both police and security reports provides an excellent base of information.

Security activity and incident reports are usually kept on file for several years in their employer's office. These reports can be of great benefit to the defense if the security service was employed to prevent the type of incident being litigated.

Evidence of regular continued patrols and inspections is critical to demonstrate that the business operator was attempting to fulfill the legal duty of providing adequate security. Poorly written or incomplete security reports can prove damaging to a defendant, especially if the reports display obvious patterns of criminal activity with no evidence of a corrective response.

Larger companies and corporations with regional security personnel develop periodic crime summaries and statistical analysis for their management. These documents will not only show criminal activity for a particular property but often will rank and compare it to other similar operations within the organization.

Security reports usually have to be obtained via subpoena and should be specifically named, if possible. A two year minimum sampling of reports up to the date of the incident is recommended. Similar to police crime reports, reports written after the incident involved are generally not admissible.

Size of Relevant Crime Radius

Establishing the crime history of a physical site is always important. For the evaluation of crime foreseeability and prior notice issues, it is helpful to research crime records for the surrounding area to determine what level of criminal activity is present in the same environment as the property involved in litigation.

By obtaining this data, it can be determined whether the premises in question is operating with a higher, lower, or similar crime experience than other property in the same area. This assumes that the surrounding area has a comparable population density and similar premises types.

In some cases of either very high or low crime records on-site, the crime records off-site will become less relevant. For example, any reasonable person should conclude that one armed robbery per month in a convenience store is high, or that a eight year crime free history in a senior citizens apartment complex is very low. Additional records of off-site crime activity will be of little value in evaluating their security programs.

It would not be practical to set a standard radius in all cases due the vast number of variables possible. A good rule of thumb is to start with the smallest crime reporting segment available from the police and move outward as required to obtain a reasonable sampling. It may be necessary to obtain records from two separate jurisdictions if the property is situated on the city boundary line. In an urban area, a smaller local sampling of four blocks in all directions may be more relevant.

Of importance is what area around the site is considered to be its environment. An environment for a business is the area from which it draws the majority of its business. Depending on the nature of the business, that area could be several blocks, several miles, or somewhere in between.

An environment for a residential or lodging facility is more likely to be only the immediate neighborhood of several blocks. However, when evaluating the robbery history of a convenience store located on a major thoroughfare, it may be more useful to research the robbery history of similar businesses along the same route for one half mile in each direction rather than a residential community immediately surrounding the site.

The evaluation of crime history for an apartment complex in a high density rental community would benefit more from research within the residential blocks immediately adjacent to the property rather than in a nearby commercial area.

Relevant Crime Types

The issue of what crime types may be relevant at trial is often disputed in premises liability litigation. Courts have been inconsistent at best in establishing guidelines. Some jurisdictions still cling to the "prior similars" rule of allowing only crime history similar to the incident being litigated. In California, New York, Florida, and other states, other less obvious crime types have been ruled admissible as long as their relevance could be shown. In general, however, only stranger-to-stranger crimes against persons are true indicators of future assaultive crime probability. Most studies conducted to date have found little direct correlation between property crime patterns and foreseeability of assaultive crime.

In a hypothetical case involving a hotel parking lot robbery and assault, certainly all stranger-to-stranger crimes against persons in the parking structure should be relevant. An argument might be made for including all automobile thefts, burglaries, and vandalism, claiming that criminals are on the grounds, and that hotel guests are exposed to them when using the hotel's parking structure.

What about crimes against persons inside the hotel? What about room burglaries? They might be admissible under the argument of a general security maintenance problem.

In a shopping center environment, shoplifting thefts should be excluded from evidence in a case involving a stabbing incident in the parking lot, on the grounds of relevancy. However, those same shoplifting statistics should be deemed relevant to a stabbing incident outside of a store involving an attempt by store personnel to apprehend a thief.

In a premises liability litigation for criminal acts of third parties, usually only stranger-to-stranger crimes against persons are relevant. Other property crimes and disturbances of the peace on the premises may become relevant if it can be demonstrated that a potential for escalation to violent crime existed.

This is usually accomplished through use of witness testimony to the effect that police statistics do not reflect the true nature of the premises. For example, a local tavern may have the reputation for frequent fights and assaults, which are unreported to the police. Witness testimony may support the argument for including certain property crime reports that are relevant to the litigation.

Domestic violence and other assaults between spouses and acquaintances might be viewed as not foreseeable, since assaults between spouses and friends are not often preventable except by physical security measures. Domestic violence (including acquaintances) was not consistently classified as a crime until recent years.

Relevant Crime Location

Proximity of prior crimes can sometimes be more relevant than the type of crime. For example, let us assume that one apartment building out of fifteen in a large complex has been the subject of more than thirty percent of the total vandalisms and burglaries in the complex. Even though there is an absence of prior assaultive crimes in this building, evidence of prior property crimes should be relevant because of the concentration of crime and notice to the landlord.

The location or area of control of the business operator can make a difference as to which crimes are relevant. For example, shopping mall security guards have control over the common areas such as the parking lots and walkways. Assaultive crimes committed inside individual leased shops may not be deemed relevant to an allegation of security negligence for failure to prevent an assault in the parking lot.

Field Interviews

It is impossible to evaluate crime foreseeability or determine if security was adequate on a premises from behind a desk. One or more visits to the site and surrounding neighborhood are required to gain an understanding of the environment. This environment may be impacted by a school, a shopping center, a sports stadium, or park. This impact may be daily, nightly, or only on a scheduled basis. These special circumstances must be considered in the over-all review process.

In addition to the site survey, there should be field interviews conducted of property inhabitants, employees, neighbors, and local businesses. (These interviews should not be conducted with employees named as defendant's by a plaintiff without prior permission.) The purpose of this interview process is to locate potential witnesses, gain feed-back on the reputation of the premises, and validate the probative value of police crime records. Investigators, rather than security expert's, should be used for this task to protect the attorney-client privilege.

Although personal interviews are subjective in nature, one can obtain a better picture on how others view their environment. Proper questioning techniques can usually separate fact from fiction and personal knowledge from hearsay. In the event that crime records are unavailable, these field interviews may be an important ingredient for assessing crime foreseeability.

Opening or closing of a high school, shopping center, movie theater, or recreation park nearby can have a major impact on crime activity on a property. This condition may weaken the value of crime statistics. New owners or management have been known to significantly alter the nature of a business and therefore its future crime potential. Sometimes reviewing crime statistics before and after a change in business status will clearly reflect the effect of the change on the crime activity.

Locating and interviewing police beat officers who patrol the property should be standard procedure. These police officers can be either favorable or unfavorable witnesses. Attorneys should find this out well in advance of any trial to avoid being surprised later. Police officers are usually viewed as experts by a jury and can be key witnesses in a trial. If crime records are only available for a larger geographic area than desired, these beat officers can be extremely valuable in isolating the high and low crime pockets.

Police officers who are familiar with the day-to-day operation of a premises will often be well qualified to comment on crime problems they have encountered. In addition, most police officers have their own opinion on the relative security of the site compared to other similar locations in their reporting area.

Conclusion

Crime demographics alone can indicate crime foreseeability independent of the other two factors, location and nature of the premises, by the existence of prior assaultive crime on the site.

Local crime records and witness testimony are usually the best indicators of future crime potential. The identification of the quantitative as well as qualitative components of the crime demographics will aid the evaluation of both foreseeability and security adequacy issues.

Lack of demographic information will not automatically preclude a finding of foreseeability of crime, especially in the case of a new business. Consideration of the two other factors, location and nature of the premises, will help to evaluate the elements of crime foreseeability.

Endnotes

1. Federal Bureau of Investigation, *Uniform Crime Reports, Crime in the United States* (Washington, DC: U. S. Department of Justice, F. B. I.). Published annually.
2. Bureau of Justice Statistics, *National Crime Survey, Criminal Victimization in the U. S.* (Washington, DC: U. S. Department of Justice)

CHAPTER SEVEN

Location of the Premises

Commercial real estate experts will tell you that there are only three points to consider when selecting a site for a business: location, location, and location. Most will advise that high visibility on a major thoroughfare with good accessibility is good for business. The same advice about a good location is given for residential and rental housing owners.

Nearby schools, shopping centers, and major transportation routes make certain communities more desirable for housing than others. However, the same features that may be attractive and desirable may also have the potential for increased liability.

The location of the premises is the third *factor* to be considered when evaluating crime foreseeability. Its relative importance is generally subject to what has been found through investigation of the other factors, nature of the premises and crime demographics. Of the three factors, location will usually raise the least substantial initial determination of assaultive crime foreseeability.

Location is the most likely to be influenced by conditions, for example: its relative proximity to other businesses; the nature of the business; the type of clientele drawn to the business; the surrounding population density and economic status; and its level of criminal activity.

However, location alone can sometimes indicate high crime potential. For example, almost any late night retail business located in an economically depressed area of a large city is exposed to assaultive crime potential on its property.

Location analysis must also be site specific. Crime locations must be evaluated from within a site. For example, an assault in an apartment complex can take place on the second floor of a building, the rear parking lot, or inside the recreation room. Certain locations within a property will be safer than others.

It is important to consider various ways to look at the location factor as it relates to assaultive crime foreseeability.

Location Within a State

A statewide evaluation of crime potential is of little benefit in determining crime foreseeability for a particular property. Although some cities within a state may have a reputation for higher crime than others, this information does not provide sufficient data to evaluate crime foreseeability.

Most urban cities with populations over one hundred thousand will typically have a higher crime rate in raw numbers when compared to their rural counterparts. For example, the national robbery rate in 1987 averaged 213 robberies per 100,000 people.

In metropolitan areas, the robbery rate was 269; in cities outside metropolitan areas, it was 50; and in the rural areas, it was 15. With 900 robberies per 100,000 inhabitants, the highest rates were recorded in cities with populations over one million.[1]

In our mobile society, a business located in a rural area but on a major highway approaching a major city will have an increased potential for robberies and assaults because of its location and accessibility.

Will a person be more likely to become victimized by a violent crime in a large metropolitan city than in a smaller community? The answer is, statistically, yes. However, each location within the state must be viewed on a case by case basis and evaluated for the elements and conditions that might indicate an increased crime potential.

Location Within a City

Most cities with populations greater than 100,000 have pockets within them that would be considered high crime locations. To say that cities like New York, Los Angeles, and Miami are high crime locations offers us little insight as to the crime foreseeability level of a particular property within these cities.

This reputation is often subjective and relative to the crime rates of other parts of the city. High crime compared to what? Certainly there are areas within each of these cities that have relatively low crime rates. Sometimes 80 percent of the total crime can be attributed to only 20 percent of a city's geography.

In an article on criminal behavior, C. Ray Jeffery concluded:

One gets an entirely different feel for crime rates if one looks at national, regional or state data, compared to block data or even individual crime site data. Bullock (1955) discovered that murders in Houston occurred along four streets. Feeney (1973) discovered that 25% of the robberies occurred in 4% of the city; in the case of commercial robbery all occurred within 12% of the city. An analysis of crime by census tracts, state, regional, or national units reveal certain interesting things about crime rate, but they mask the relationship of crime to the physical environment. If one bar has all the murders and 50% of the robberies, we want to study that one bar, not the murder rate for the city of Los Angeles or the state of California.[2]

Larger cities usually have sections designated as industrial, commercial, residential, or some combination of each. If crimes against persons were mapped with a colored dot or pin positioned at the site on a city map, a pattern of activity would emerge.

The emergent pattern is of no surprise to most law enforcement agencies. A common pattern would show assaultive crime activity where large groups of people congregate, for example, shopping centers, apartment complexes, sports stadiums, housing projects, and public parks.

Major thoroughfares lined with retail stores can show a straight-line pattern of criminal activity and assaults for a mile or more following the commercial outlets, while the adjacent neighborhoods along the way are relatively unaffected.

Location Within a Neighborhood

A particular property can have crime problems based on its relation to other businesses and premises types. For example, a rather subdued furniture store located in a busy shopping plaza can be affected by the traffic and crime problems created by the other, more volatile, retail tenants.

Criminal activity on a commercial property is often affected by its proximity to schools and residential neighborhoods.

Oscar Newman concluded in a study that:

> there is also evidence suggesting that both younger and poorer criminals operate in areas close to their homes; most crimes in moderate and low-income residential areas are committed by teenagers who live nearby.[3]

Another location consideration is the volume of both vehicle and foot traffic in and around the property, especially at night. Convenience stores, gas stations, and fast food outlets are affected most by this characteristic.

In 1969, Shlomo Angel conducted a mapping study of the incidence of crime in Oakland, California. He found that most crimes occurred where there was either a very small or very large volume of traffic. He concluded that there is a "critical intensity zone," and that the "right amount" of traffic is a deterrent to crime. The right amount provides for enough people to notice a crime but not so many that no one will take it upon himself to intervene.[4]

Ease of access of a particular location has proven to be a factor in the level of crime on a premises. Whether a store is located at a four-way intersection, on major thoroughfares, or has high or low traffic counts makes a difference as to its crime foreseeability. Corner locations are often victimized because they provide better escape routes.

In a study published by Bevis and Nutter[5], an analysis of street intersections was made. A cross intersection, "+," was considered the most accessible; streets that formed "T" and "L" shaped intersections were considered less accessible. Researcher Luedtke[6] and others have found that stores on or near a corner have a higher probability of being burglarized than stores in the interior blocks.

Proximity to freeway on-ramps and expressways can be an important factor when escape by vehicle is part of the criminal's plan. The number of signal lights, stop signs, and even the speed limit can affect a decision to use a particular street as an escape route. In addition, the location of a business on a one-way street or on a street with raised medians restricting traffic flow to one direction is sometimes weighed by a criminal before choosing a site for a criminal act.

Location Within a Premises

Certain locations within a premises can have a higher degree of crime foreseeability than others, based on the elements of accessibility, opportunities for concealment, and availability of escape routes.

Many apartment complexes, for example, will report a higher rate of burglary, prowling, and sexual assaults for ground floor units compared to units on upper floors. Units toward the rear of an apartment complex lacking surveillance opportunities by other tenants or street traffic often have more crime as well.

Commercial offices and retail stores located in first floor free-standing buildings with immediate access to the street or parking lot are more likely to be affected by robberies and assaults. Those with an element such as restricted or no visibility by the public or other tenants are the more probable targets. Conditions such as large amounts of cash or easily sold merchandise on hand will increase the exposure to criminal assault.

A shopping center will generally have a higher assaultive crime foreseeability level in its parking lots and common areas than inside crowded stores. Occasionally, one small section or level of a shopping center parking lot can account for the majority of the assaultive crimes due to its proximity to an exit or major thoroughfare.

When all employees park their vehicles in a particular location every work day, it makes it easier for an assailant to select a target, and limits foot traffic around those vehicles during business hours.

Conditions that can impact the crime foreseeability level of a particular location can be the level of illumination at night, amount of surveillance opportunities, amount of visibility, noise level, accessibility, frequency of police or security guard patrol, effectiveness of the security devices and hardware in place, effectiveness of other crime prevention procedures, weather, temperature, and any other intervening variable that might affect the function of an element of crime foreseeability.

As with the other two factors, nature of the premises and crime demographics, conditions can impact the location factor in a positive way as well. For example, excellent levels of illumination, good visibility, cash handling procedures, an adequate number of trained staff, video cameras and other devices, and robbery prevention training can reduce the potential of robbery of a convenience store in even the most volatile locations.

Conclusion

The mere location of a premises alone can indicate that assaultive crime is indeed foreseeable. The consideration of the other two factors, nature of the premises and crime demographics, will either mitigate or aggravate the initial finding based on the location factor. Evaluating the impact of the location factor and its conditions is very important since crime can be affected greatly by them.

Endnotes

1. Federal Bureau of Investigation, *Uniform Crime Reports, Crime in the United States* (Washington, D. C.: U. S. Department of Justice, F. B. I., 1987), 17.
2. C. Ray Jeffery, "Criminal Behavior and the Physical Environment," *American Behavioral Scientist* 20, 2 (1976): 166-167.
3. Oscar Newman, *Design Guidelines for Creating Defensible Space* (Washington, D. C.: U. S. Department of Justice, Law Enforcement Assistance Administration, National Institute of Law Enforcement and Criminal Justice, 1976), 35.
4. Shlomo Angel, *Discouraging Crime Through City Planning* (Berkeley, Calif.: University of California, Institute of Urban and Regional Development, Center for Planning & Development, Working Paper No. 75, 1968).
5. Herb Rubenstein, *et al., The Link Between Crime and the Built Environment: The Current State of Knowledge* (Washington, D. C.: U. S. Department of Justice, National

Institute of Justice, 1980), 35, quoting from C. Bevis and J. B. Nutter, *Changing Street Layouts to Reduce Residential Burglary* (St Paul, Minn.: Governor's Commission of Crime Prevention and Control, 1977).
6. *Ibid.*, 36, quoting from Luedtke and Associates, *Crime and the Physical City* (Detroit, Mich.: Luedtke and Associates, 1970), respectively.

ADEQUACY OF SECURITY

CHAPTER EIGHT

Evaluation for Adequacy

In premises liability litigation, the adequacy of security evaluation is of primary interest to all parties. Because various aspects of security are commonly in dispute, the ambiguity of the term "adequacy" often complicates the discussions. It is crucial, therefore, to establish a clear understanding of the term in this context if the actual evaluation is to be meaningful.

Attempts have been made in various court cases to clarify misconceptions and confusion concerning the term "adequate security."

In *7735 Hollywood Blvd. Venture v. Superior Court*, the court commented:

> It would be intolerable and grossly unfair to permit a lay jury, after the fact, to determine in any case that security measures were "inadequate," especially in light of the fact that the decision would always be rendered in a

case where the security had in fact proved to be inadequate.[1]

The practice of using security experts to provide opinion testimony as to the adequacy of security after the fact also came under fire from the same court, for the similar reasons.

In *Noble v. Los Angeles Dodgers*, the court added:

> It appears that a growth industry is developing consisting of experts who will advise and testify as to what, in their opinion, constitutes "adequate security." The $64 question, of course, is "adequate for what?" As noted, in each case where such testimony would be relevant, the security in existence has already proven to be inadequate to prevent the injury which did occur. The question then to be determined by the jury is what reasonable steps could have been taken to prevent plaintiff's injury? The purpose of a trial in this type of case is not simply to critique defendant's security measures and to compare them to some abstract standards espoused by a so-called "security expert."[2]

While some incompetent expert evaluations and "hired guns" are undoubtedly to be found in the field of security negligence litigation, the above criticism by the court neither makes the specialty unique, nor does it negate the value of a properly carried out evaluation. On the contrary, it points to a need for definition and methodology to clear up the ambiguity in the issues.

In this type of litigation, then, the test of adequacy of security is not whether the security was adequate to prevent a given offense, but whether the level of security was a reasonable fulfillment of the landowner's duty of care. In many situations, foreseeability does impose a duty on the landowner to exercise a reasonable level of care without specifying the level needed.

It is precisely these tensions in the case law that give rise to the need for a test that balances the entire condition of the property against the level of crime foreseeability, rather than one that merely asks whether certain devices were present.

The objective, then, is to determine whether a particular defendant should, under the circumstances, be held liable for a plaintiff's injury, not necessarily because of a failure to prevent the criminal actions of a third party, but because of a failure to implement sufficient and reasonable security measures.

In this chapter, we will discuss the process of evaluating whether a security program in place at a given location was adequate to prevent the occurrence of foreseeable criminal acts. We will also define and outline evaluation criteria, which, when applied objectively, will yield a complete analysis that can be presented to a jury.

Without a consistent methodology in mind, neither the security expert nor the attorney will be able to develop a complete and thorough analysis of the case. The evaluation criteria presented here enable one to identify and analyze all relevant factors and develop an opinion supported by facts, statistics, and effective security industry practices. Only then can a jury be expected to view this analysis as objective and credible, and apply significant weight to it.

The discussion here is designed to illustrate a method by which an expert analysis of security may be constructed, and to make the method understandable to those not acquainted with the field. Our intent is not to teach security methods nor is it to endorse any standards.

It is important to understand that adequacy of security issues must be evaluated on a case by case basis. Each case generally has enough significant idiosyncrasies to render a "cookbook" evaluation, based on universal standards and practices, invalid.

Our focus in applying evaluation criteria is on relevant security measures as they relate to specific criminal acts, that is, on assaultive crimes or crimes that engender victimization.

In addition, one should not restrict an evaluation to the security measures that may have had the most obvious connection to the incident. The entire program must be evaluated to determine whether a more efficient combination of resources would have resulted in a significantly greater reduction of the probability of future harm.

Before evaluating security for adequacy is discussed, we must first define the terminology.

What is Adequate?

According to Webster's dictionary, "adequate" is defined as (1) sufficient for a specific requirement, and (2) lawfully and reasonably sufficient.

The word "reasonable" is defined as (1) not conflicting with reason, (2) not extreme or excessive.

The word "sufficient" is defined as (1) enough to meet the needs of a situation or a proposed end.[3]

What is Security?

For our purposes, security is defined as a method of protecting persons and property from criminal acts through the use of operational, physical, and technical crime prevention resources. These resources are directed at both reducing the attractiveness of potential targets and making them more difficult to attack, "hardening the target."

Because the requirements for a criminal to commit a crime and crime foreseeability levels are related, determining the adequacy of security is somewhat like evaluating from a criminal's point of view. In order to evaluate security, one must first have an understanding of the basic requirements necessary to commit a criminal act.

They are (1) motivation, (2) possession of necessary skills and tools, and (3) opportunity. Attempts to learn what motivates criminals have been the subject matter of many studies. It is not possible to present here an authoritative rule of thumb that simply and easily answers the question of what motivates different classes of criminals. However, motivation can be defined here as the varying levels of interest, desire, and need to commit a particular crime.

Highly motivated criminals will wait for the precise opportunity, and make repeated attempts at the target, and not be deterred by the consequences of apprehension.

In addition to motivation are the skills and tools possessed by the criminal. The level of skill a criminal obtains generally rises to meet the level of motivation. Skills may include special knowledge or training on how to circumvent security hardware such as locks and alarm systems or how to penetrate upper floors of a building. Skills may also include the ability to adapt to an environment and to use deception to circumvent detection by casual observers, security patrols, or facility staff.

Tools utilized in crime can be as simple and inexpensive as a screwdriver or as highly sophisticated as a portable hydraulic door frame jack. The application of a sophisticated tool against a security measure generally requires a higher degree of motivation and skill.

In a premises liability litigation, most criminal assaults are the result of relatively unsophisticated criminals, who require only average to below average skill and motivation. Because of this, as the level of motivation and tools used by a criminal increases the ability to foresee such crimes decreases proportionately.

Opportunity is where a criminal finds it, for example, an open door, a lone female in a dark parking lot, a defective sliding glass door latch, or poor cash handling policies in a convenience store. Opportunity may exist for only brief periods or continue for an extended time.

In our open society, opportunity for crime is everywhere. Opportunity can only be reduced by security precautions and by general and individual (specific) deterrence measures. The most common way in which a security system can address deterrence is by reducing the physical opportunity for crime.

Hardening a premises can be effective in reducing the crime opportunity and therefore raising the level of motivation and sophistication of skills and tools required to gain entry. The level of basic motivation in many criminals is low enough that rudimentary security measures, designed to reduce the criminal's perception of a situation as an opportunity for crime, will also succeed in deterrence. Occasionally, a business owner can prevent crimes simply by placing barriers in the path of the criminal and by increasing the likelihood of the crime being observed.

The Three-Way Test

Usually, premises liability lawsuits claim that a landowner owed a duty of care to its land entrants to protect them from harm from foreseeable criminal acts, and that the breach of this duty was the proximate cause of their client's injury.

Assuming that a duty existed, the evaluation of whether security was reasonable (adequate) or not, should balance three criteria. When used together during the evaluation process, these criteria become a *three-way test* for adequacy of security.

The three evaluation criteria are (1) the level of crime foreseeability, (2) the likelihood that a given combination of security measures will prevent future harm, and (3) the burden of taking such precautions against crime.

The determination of whether security is reasonable or not depends on the interrelation of these three factors. A high level of crime foreseeability will require security measures that meet a stricter test of the likelihood of prevention of future harm at a cost that is not prohibitive. A low level of crime foreseeability may only require minimal security precautions, many of which may be addressed by hardware and procedures alone.

These evaluation criteria should be of equal interest to both plaintiff and defense counsels. If applied fairly, the strong and weak points on each side will be identified.

Law of the Hammer

The significance of applying this three-way test is that it challenges attorneys and their experts to make responsible evaluations of whether security in place was in fact adequate, given the requirements of a particular situation. This leads to evaluations that are based on reasonableness rather than on a fantasy of radical, high-tech security systems or armies of security guards on every type property.

The tendency of this three-way test toward moderation may counteract the "law of the hammer," a doctrine which translates to "when a boy finds a hammer, he finds that everything he encounters needs pounding."[4] In many litigation cases every possible security measure gets "pounded," regardless of its efficacy in preventing future crimes.

Public Policy

Public policy is an expression of the discretion often exercised by the court to justify unreasonable measures. For example, a court ruling that validates a requirement for a minimum number of security personnel at all nighttime fast food outlets would place an enormous burden on an entire industry, many of which would not benefit from the requirement. This type of across-the-board ruling would definitely be against public policy and normally does not pass the appellate court.

Another result of the three-way test is the elimination of the argument that if a needed level of security is too costly to provide, the land possessor need not provide beyond his ability to do so. Due to the high costs of adding significant security measures to a high crime location, some land possessors have failed to take any crime prevention steps.

In such cases, the reluctant party could have decided to either change the nature of the business, relocate, modify current business practices, cease doing business, or do nothing and accept the liability for inadequate security.

The final option is contrary to public policy, and thus the three-way test does not allow for it. Attempting to transfer liability to lessees or insurance carriers may satisfy certain financial issues but not the responsibility resulting from a legal duty.

Juries have made loud and clear statements to this effect to land possessors in the form of punitive damage awards to injured parties.

Level of Crime Foreseeability

The first evaluation criterion, crime foreseeability, was defined previously as being either not foreseeable, low, moderate, or high. Once a level of crime foreseeability is determined, the security precautions that existed at the time of the injury can be evaluated for their effectiveness.

Likelihood of Prevention of Future Harm

The second evaluation criterion in our three-way test is the likelihood of prevention of future harm. This criterion should help provide the answer to the $64 question, "Adequate for what?" asked by a trial judge, by acting as a test and validating the potential effectiveness and reasonableness of any combination of security measures.

The likelihood of preventing future harm can only be evaluated after first establishing a level of crime foreseeability, "where the burden of preventing future harm is great, a high degree of foreseeability may be required."[5]

Simply stated, more effective security measures are required as crime foreseeability increases.

In *7735 Hollywood Blvd. Venture, supra,* the court stated that crime "foreseeability...does not, *per se,* impose a duty on such property owners or proprietors to install a 'security device' which meets the lay jury's concept of adequacy,"[6] when in actuality little benefit resulted from a crime prevention standpoint. Thus security measures can therefore be in place, sometimes in great quantities, and still be deemed inadequate.

However, the security precaution or group of precautions in place must have a high probability of preventing the criminal activity for which they were designed. Security precautions *do not* have to be perfect. Rarely is there a security device or procedure that performs perfectly under all circumstances.

The Burden of Taking Precautions

The third factor in our three-way test focuses on the burden of providing for security and operates under the same concept of reasonableness. This burden is normally expressed in terms of added costs in hardware, equipment, and labor.

Sometimes the necessary or proposed security measures or change in the way of doing business will impact the sales or income potential of a business.

The costs of adding some security procedures can be relatively small. Even locations with low crime foreseeability would be scrutinized for not taking simple or inexpensive steps. For example, installation of entry door peepholes in residential rental units or wooden dowels for sliding glass windows would be at a very low cost per unit. By hiring a full-time security guard to patrol at night, a large hotel would add less than five cents to the cost of a room, assuming no other security measures presently exist.

The other side of the equation involves the financial unreasonableness of some security measures. For a convenience store or small liquor store to hire a full-time security guard to prevent armed robberies may be too burdensome or costly when lesser measures may be adequate and more effective.

The burden of adding certain security measures could be so cost prohibitive that it would be unreasonable and against public policy to require it. We all can visualize the image of a castle protected by a stone wall, drawbridge, and moat filled with alligators. Although most would say this level of security is probably adequate, it most likely would not pass our test of reasonableness, as defined.

The courts have declined to declare a duty whose imposition:

> would place an extremely onerous burden on both the defendant and the community, and where the defendant is not morally culpable, and where the proposed duty and the measures to be applied in discharge of the duty defy exact delineation and suffer from inherent vagueness.[7]

The impact of case law on the business and insurance industry would be too great if courts allowed unreasonable standards of security to be established by jury verdicts.

Standard of Care

Often in premises liability litigation, attorneys will use the term "standard of care." This term is sometimes confusing because it indicates that some standard or precise measure exists. In the security industry very few standards exist. What does exist are security precautions commonly used by the industry with a high degree of effectiveness. However, any number of precautions applied in a variety of ways can be effective in combating assaultive crime. Our focus here is the legal standard of care of reasonableness and effectiveness in applying security methodology.

Testing for Effectiveness

Evidence of effectiveness can sometimes be found by checking compliance with building codes and ordinances, and compliance with the security standards, or common practices adopted and used effectively in the industry.

Door locking hardware found not in compliance with the building security codes, where adopted, will be viewed as inadequate in most cases, if it is established that compliance would likely prevent an assailant's entry.

Hardware and equipment are relatively easy to test for adequacy because of existing testing standards and manufacturer specifications. See Chapter Ten. Hardware and equipment either work according to or near specifications or they do not.

Crime Deterrents

The difficult security precautions to evaluate are those that are alleged to have a crime deterrent effect. Some precautions are considered physical deterrents while others are psychological deterrents. Some are considered general deterrents while others are specific deterrents. An example of a general physical crime deterrent would be an unsupervised barrier such as an eight foot high chain link fence with three-strand barbed wire on top. A specific crime deterrent would be the application of a security guard to control a single access portal to a parking garage.

Potential psychological deterrents may include a well lighted area, periodic patrols by a uniformed security guard, a procedure of keeping less than $30 in a convenience store cash register at night, security warning signage, video surveillance cameras, and a lack of escape routes.

These deterrents are only effective on alert, sober, and receptive criminals who are affected by the possibility of being observed, apprehended, and punished.

A example of a deterrent effect would be a situation where most auto thieves will be deterred because of the integration of parking structure design, high visibility, access control using parking tickets, toll booth barrier egress, and use of video cameras with communication and response personnel. This level of security precautions would probably be deemed adequate to protect against most auto thefts and other related crimes.

In contrast, good lighting has little deterrent effect if surveillance opportunities are absent. Security guard access control is ineffective if the person is untrained and not supervised. Video cameras are of little benefit if phony or obviously not monitored by anyone.

Chain link fences offer little resistance if a large hole in the mesh exists. Security guard patrols are ineffective if they conform to a set schedule or are not highly visible.

Any of the above security deterrents could be integrated into a premises and still be deemed ineffective because of poor application of the measure. Therefore, it is important to evaluate the effect of any potential deterrent before assuming that the security in place is adequate.

Conclusion

The term "adequate" for our purposes of evaluating security precautions is inherently vague and meaningless until clearly defined. The concept of adequate security becomes clear when we apply the "three-way test" evaluation criteria to the issues at hand and balance our findings in a fair and reasonable manner. Only then can an objective opinion be rendered that is based on relevant facts, actual effectiveness, and reasonableness.

Endnotes

1. *7735 Hollywood Blvd. Venture v. Superior Court*, 116 Cal.App.3d 910, 172 Cal.Rptr. 528 (1981), 530.
2. *Noble v. Los Angeles Dodgers*, 168 Cal.App.3d 912, 214 Cal.Rptr. 395 (1985) 398.
3. *Webster's Ninth New Collegiate Dictionary, s. v.* "adequate," "reasonable," and "sufficient."
4. Abraham Kaplin, *Conduct of Inquiry* (San Francisco, Calif.: Chandler Publishing Co., 1964).
5. *Gomez v. Ticor*, 145 Cal.App.3d 622, 193 Cal. Rptr. 600 (1983), 605.
6. *Hollywood, supra*, 530.
7. *Cohen v. Southland Corporation*, 157 Cal.App.3d 130, 203 Cal.Rptr. 572 (1984), 578.

CHAPTER NINE

Evaluation of Security

In this chapter we will discuss how to evaluate the relative effectiveness of various security precautions on a particular premises. In the security profession, some security precautions have demonstrated that they will prevent certain crimes more effectively than others. Conversely, the effectiveness of those same crime prevention methods can vary depending on the nature and location of the premises and the types of crimes to be impacted.

Before we begin a discussion of how to evaluate security effectiveness, we need to define the terminology being used. Throughout this section we will be using terms such as "deter" and "prevent."

Webster's dictionary defines "deter" as to turn aside, to discourage, or prevent from acting. The word "prevent" is defined as to be in readiness for, to meet, or satisfy in advance.[1]

For our purposes, both words describe the same potential concept of stopping crimes before they are committed.

A significant difference is that "prevent" in the security industry usually describes those security precautions designed in advance to physically stop certain crimes from occurring. For example, solid doors with adequate locks will physically prevent most assailants from entering and causing harm to the occupant. A doorman or security guard controlling access to a high rise building will prevent most assailants from penetrating upper floors by denying access to them. A nighttime personal escort service for female workers from their place of employment to their vehicles will prevent most assaults.

The word "deter" used in the security industry is less concrete. Good illumination in a parking lot may deter criminals for fear of observation. A security guard patrol may deter a prowler in an apartment complex who needs privacy. A high fence may deter a burglar who requires a quick escape route. In each of these situations the criminal will not be physically stopped but hopefully will think twice about committing the crime.

In some environments, both words are descriptive of the effectiveness of security. In a convenience store, for example, a time delayed cash drop safe and good cash handling policies can both prevent robberies of large amounts of money and may deter future robberies because of having only small amounts of cash on hand in the register.

Both words used in the security industry allow for the potential of some crime to occur regardless of the amount of security precautions in place. Unfortunately, no security precaution is perfect. All crimes cannot be prevented or deterred.

On a property open to the public, it is difficult to prevent crimes against persons because of the personal freedom that everyone expects. Often the best that can be accomplished is to have a high visibility deterrent, using both physical and psychological security methods in a hope that a criminal will choose another location to victimize. This deterrent effect, however, is only effective if the criminal is coherent, rational, and sober enough to be able to recognize the security deterrent in place.

When evaluating for security effectiveness one must assume that criminals have the capability to make rational assessments. No security program could function in the private sector if it had to address its security precautions to irrational or insane persons. It seems impractical to attempt to evaluate the deterrent effects on those incapable of interpreting them.

Criminologists label these deterrants as either a general or individual (specific) deterrent when the criminal may be affected by the possibility of being apprehended and punished and therefore not react to the opportunity.

A seventeenth century judge expressed this idea of specific deterrence when he sentenced a man to death for horse stealing. He said, "I am not sending you to hang because you stole a horse. I am hanging you so horses might not be stolen."[2]

Many criminologists also believe that most crime prevention and crime deterrence methods only serve to move the criminal to another location or time period. This has been called the crime displacement or hydraulic theory.[3] Others believe that some crimes are opportunistic, and if prevented, will not necessarily occur again unless another opportunity presents itself.

A business operator may be extremely successful in reducing criminal assaults by preventing and deterring them from occurring. However, considering the concept of crime displacement, it is reasonable to expect that crimes will begin to return to a premises when security precautions are discontinued or when existing hardware and equipment are not maintained. For that reason questions should be asked regarding previous levels of security compared to those in place at the time of the incident.

Security Methodology

There are four areas of security methodology that are generally considered to combat crime. They are (1) facility design, (2) personnel, (3) hardware, and (4) procedures.

What follows will be a review of practical applications for each area of security methodology and a discussion on how each area should be viewed for its crime prevention effectiveness.

Keep in mind that often we have to evaluate the effectiveness of a combination of all methods listed above. Security methods used in combination will often have a synergistic effect, and may prevent or deter a wider variety of crimes than any single application.

A Word About Standards

In the security industry it is difficult to find many standards. The word "standard" implies that a definite rule or principle is established by some authority and can be used as a means of measurement or comparison.

Standard security packaging has been tried for a number of industries (e.g., convenience stores, department stores, hotel chains, and the federal government). Most packaged security programs are doomed to fail due to the number of unique variables for each business and at each location, although the original concept may have been acceptable on a test site and for a given period of time. Problems commonly arise because company policies are not fully enforced; layout and floor plans change; crime vulnerability changes; and technology changes. Some modifications are always required to address unique issues.

Electronic security equipment has an ageing problem and is usually the first to become obsolete, oftentimes within a period of several years. A standard established two years ago may be antiquated and now substandard because of changes to the environment.

The problem of dictating a standard to the private sector is a complex issue. What authority would set the standards—the government, the police, or some special security commission? Would there be different standards for higher crime areas? Would the standards be retroactive? Who would be exempt? Who would enforce the standards?

The solution to date has been to back away from the restrictive concept of gauging by some standard. Most properties are secured today by the guideline of commonly used practices. As stated previously, certain security precautions have been commonly used in the various industries for years with a high degree of success.

Trained and knowledgeable security professionals know what security methods to apply to different applications, and which methods will tend to impact assaultive crime on a property.

This information is available to the public through the security industry and some law enforcement agencies. Each site must be evaluated individually to determine the best method of adequately securing the premises.

This is accomplished by conducting a security survey of the site.

The Site Survey

A survey of the physical site is an important and necessary component in an evaluation for adequacy of security issues. The site of assaultive crime must be considered for its role in the liability issues raised by a plaintiff. This survey should be conducted by a security expert.

To be effective, the expert should have already completed the crime demographic research for the site and surrounding area. The expert should have reviewed all relevant documentation regarding the facts of the assault, be familiar with the nature of the premises, and be knowledgeable about what security equipment and procedures were in place at the time. The expert should have a general opinion of the level of crime foreseeability for the surrounding area and preliminary opinion for that of the site.

It is recommended that the attorney and business operator, or some other person who has firsthand knowledge of the actual conditions, be available to point out changes in the site. The survey should be conducted near the same time of day as the actual assault and/or in similar lighting conditions.

The actual process for conducting a security survey will vary depending on the nature of the premises, type of crime, and liability issues alleged. The site survey focuses on two of the four areas of security methodology discussed previously, facility design and hardware applications. The other two areas, personnel and procedures, are normally evaluated during the documentation review in the discovery phase.

It is important to keep in mind, however, how the level of staffing and quality of procedures would have interfaced with the physical security precautions of the site.

Simulations can be conducted on-site, if necessary, to test the effectiveness of personnel or procedures and how they interface with the equipment.

If a litigation complaint involves issues of exact measurements and location of certain equipment, it is recommended that a diagram of the property be obtained. Most experts can produce a rough diagram good enough for their file, to aid in recollection should the need arise. A professional scale diagram is necessary only when a courtroom exhibit is needed, and a high degree of accuracy is required.

Photographs of the premises, hardware, or other property attributes are highly recommended as a graphic representation of the physical security precautions in place. Photographs are frequently used at trial to supplement testimony and give the jury the same point of reference and visual image as the witness.

Facility Design

Facility design attributes are the most often overlooked aspect of a security system. The facility design alone can have a significant impact on criminal activity and ultimately on crime foreseeability. The key goals of a facility designed for security are to control access and to provide for maximum visibility.

The physical design and nature of a premises often dictate what security measures can be implemented and in what quantities. Many lawsuit allegations claiming inadequate security involve older structures between twenty and sixty years old.

At the time of their design, crime foreseeability and security were probably not at issue. The structure's design was determined by functionality and cost, with little or no priority given to security. In addition, structures constructed more than thirty years ago may have had an adequate level of security designed into the facility for that time period.

Today's Uniform Building Security Code,[4] discussed in greater detail in Chapter Ten, and other hardware standards were not adopted until the late 1970's. Building age, neighborhood decay, and increasing crime have rendered many previously secure buildings inadequate by today's standards. Unlike antiquated building codes, security code ordinances, as adopted by many cities, must be current in residential rental properties.

The security precautions reasonably available to a premises will vary by business type. Some facilities are accessible 24-hours a day, while others operate for limited hours. Some are semiprivate, while others are open to the public.

The premises can enhance or deter criminal activity by the very nature of its design. Convenience stores, for example, are small in size and allow for quick ingress/egress to the store. Since this is a desired design feature both for the customer and the armed robber, other security measures must be applied.

A crime demographics survey may establish that armed robberies have a moderate degree of foreseeability. Store interior design features that may affect those crimes would be counter location, good lighting, and amount of visibility from the street.

Examples of store exterior design features to be considered that can affect escape routes are the location and number of ingress/egress points for the parking lot, use of barriers such as fences that cut off on-foot escapes, and landscaping to eliminate vehicle parking on the sides and rear of the stores.

Facility design has proven effective in residential properties such as apartment complexes and hotel/motels. Residential rental properties are considered to be semi-private, and for that reason, traffic flow is limited. This feature naturally lends itself to the design goal of limited access and can also aid in increasing visibility.

The security survey of a rental housing property should consider the number and location of ingress/egress points for the property. Fewer is better, and if access is controlled from only one street, it is relatively easy to monitor. Most criminals will think twice about the potential of getting trapped with their vehicle in a facility with only one or two egress points.

A security survey should pay special attention to all ground floor apartment units. First floor apartment and motel units in low-rise buildings are more likely to be victimized simply because of ease of access to doors and windows. After the front door, sliding glass doors and windows are the most common break-in point.

Good design considerations would include ground floor buffer zones of rugged shrubbery or landscaping to be used under exposed windows making access more difficult. This same shrubbery, however, can become a hazard if overgrown and poorly maintained, by creating concealment opportunities.

High-rise hotels and motels have an advantage in being able to control access to upper floors by having their front desk function located on the ground floor. It is far easier to control unauthorized access through a lobby and to the upper floors in a high rise than in a low rise complex spread over several acres. This is normally accomplished by preventing ingress through perimeter access doors after certain hours and by allowing access via the main lobby entrance only. Assailants usually find it too risky to attempt a crime on an upper floor with limited escape routes.

In parking lot facilities the main design consideration when surveying is ingress/egress opportunities. Parking lot criminals generally arrive by automobile to look less conspicuous and to aid their escape. Controlled egress will prevent many auto thefts, auto burglaries, and other assaultive crimes.

Exit control (egress) may be accomplished by a toll gate, raised curbs, fencing, landscaping, and other barriers. In urban parking structures, ingress by foot should be limited to supervised access points only. This may be accomplished by the installation of non-climbable chain link fences, walls, or iron bars on the first floor of multi-level structures.

Whatever the design consideration, these design attributes must be assigned "weight" as they mitigate or aggravate existing security on a property. For example, an apartment complex with only two access points from the same street can be easily monitored and sealed off by the police, if necessary. This is an undesirable feature for an assailant and should have a deterrent effect. A hole in a perimeter fence, however, may supply access and escape routes for an assailant and prevent surveillance by law enforcement because it is at the rear of a property.

Hardware and Equipment

Hardware, including equipment, is the most commonly used solution to security problems, which is evidenced by the number of security devices on the market today. Commonly used security hardware includes fences, solid doors, security glass, locking devices, and permanent lighting. Commonly used security equipment, depending on the application, includes video cameras, alarm systems, communication systems and patrol vehicles.

Although hardware is often used as a temporary solution to a more complex problem, it certainly has its place in crime prevention. Properly selected and installed hardware can reduce opportunities, and require greater skills and motivation on the part of the criminal to commit the act. Less commonly recognized is the fact that security hardware must be supported by personnel and procedures if it is to remain effective. The best security in the world is ineffective if a door is left standing open or a video surveillance system is unmonitored.

The failure of security hardware is a common allegation in premises liability complaints. Security hardware defects most often cited are (1) locks on doors, (2) sliding glass doors, and (3) windows. Defective lighting is the next largest area for complaints. Cases involving a defect in high tech equipment such as alarm and video systems are less prevalent.

Aside from the specific issue of defective hardware or equipment are the general allegations of inadequate security for the entire premises. These complaints sometimes allege the absence of a fence, a gate, locks on common area doors, intercom systems, video systems, lighting, or any combination of absences as the proximate cause of an assault.

During the site survey all relevant door and window locking hardware should be examined. The most commonly used devices are locking dead latch knobsets, dead bolts, surface slide bolts, and security chains. The absence or presence of any previous pry marks or obvious attempts at forced entry should be noted. On-site tests should be conducted, if possible, on any hardware specifically named in the allegation as being defective.

The hardware should be photographed in detail before and after any testing. Photographs should be of the highest quality, using a macro lens for close up shots. These photographs are often used at trial to depict the defect or absence of defect.

Testing of door or window locking hardware will cause it to either pass or fail the test. Failure of a strength test does not automatically prove liability. It is still necessary to show that the apparent defect or weakness in the hardware was the proximate cause of the assault and subsequent injury. For example, door locking hardware is found to be in working order. However, a warped door makes it difficult to close and determine if the door is actually locked. In this case, a repeated simulation is required to determine if the door will lock after reasonable attempts to secure it.

This condition is not the same as a lock defect, if reasonable attempts to secure the door would have been successful. Prior notification to the landlord of the sticky door could change this condition to a defect, if not repaired within a reasonable period. The exception to this would include the common area entry door that is designed to be self-closing and self-locking. Because of its design to be self-locking, a sticky door could be considered a defect in this case.

Sliding glass door latches in apartment and condominum units are often the focus of a case. Again, established testing criteria will determine their suitability. The addition of frame pins, thumb screws, burglar bars, and wooden dowels to the sliding glass door or window track all have proven some effectiveness in preventing access into an apartment. However, the additional security device combined with the door latch must still pass the test criteria for preventing unauthorized access.

Fences

Fences around a property serve two purposes: (1) to mark the property line, and (2) to act as a barrier to keep people and animals out. In premises liability matters the issue of a fence usually involves its ability to protect a property and its inhabitants from outside access.

For our purposes we will consider chain link, wood, cinder block, and cement walls all in the same category. The original design purpose may have been for privacy, as a wind or noise barrier, or for security purposes. Regardless of the design purpose, all fences provide some level of protection.

The most common height for a fence is either six or eight feet. All are considered to be climbable. A common application for perimeter security is a six foot chain link fence with three-strand barbed wire set onto eighteen inch outriggers installed at a forty-five degree angle toward the direction of threat. Although still considered as climbable, this design will usually keep out more than ninety percent of intruders.

During a site survey where general inadequate security is alleged, fences need to be examined. Walking the entire perimeter fence line will determine the condition and any breach points in the fence. Obvious holes in a fence with well-travelled trails leading up to them are an indication of a long term condition.

The relative importance of the condition of the fence depends on the property type, and what type of properties are on the other side of a fence. There are no real testing criteria for fences. Visual inspection and some hands-on manipulation will provide enough information as to the adequacy of any fence.

Gates attached to fencing are easy to evaluate. They are also the weakest point in a fence if they are left standing open. Security gates should be self-closing and self-locking. Visual inspection will show if methods to defeat the self-closing system or self-locking system have been utilized. Like any door locking hardware, the suitability of the lock is relevant as well its condition.

Apartment houses sometimes use intercom systems with magnetic door lock release hardware. The site survey should verify the condition and function of the system. Since this site survey is after the fact, someone else will have to testify to the actual conditions of the equipment at the time of an incident. Intercom and remote door release systems can be effective in keeping out most unwanted entrants, if they are in good working order and other tenants are security conscious.

One weakness in these systems is that unauthorized persons can gain entry to the building by walking closely behind a legitimate tenant when the door is opened (tailgating). Another major weakness is that a tenant does not know if the door is closed and locked after admitting someone by remote access.

Like any other piece of hardware, intercom systems and remote access systems must be maintained or exposure to potential liability exists.

The theory of liability applied to defective or non-performing electronic security devices is usually one of reliance. Plaintiff's may claim that the electronic device provided a false sense of security, and that they relied on that device for protection from assailants.

Lighting

Inadequate lighting is often raised as an issue in a complaint involving an assault in a parking lot or in a common area of a rental property. Lighting is often included as a supporting fact to a general count of inadequate security. To evaluate lighting as a security precaution depends on what is alleged in the complaint.

The term lighting usually refers to the number of lighting fixtures, their placement and overall effectiveness (i.e., good lighting). Illumination refers to output, brightness or intensity.

For our purposes we will discuss lighting in general, common terms. The Illuminating Engineering Society (IES) has precise measurements and terminologies, which should be referred to for more detailed information; that level of information would be too extensive for our discussion here.[5]

Outside illumination has three security purposes. They are (1) safety, (2) recognition, and (3) identification. The level of illumination required depends on the intended use and type of premises.

The first level satisfies the need to see where you are walking, to locate a vehicle in the parking lot, and to be able to insert a key into the lock.

The second level of illumination allows for recognition, at approximately one hundred feet, of a person, a dog, or other object that can be detected and alert us to any potential danger.

Level three illumination is a level of intensity where one can readily identify persons, objects and things without difficulty. At this level most people could read a sign and identify familiar faces and objects.

Aside from specialized applications, most outdoor video surveillance systems require at least level three illumination to be effective. Additional lighting fixtures can provide much more illumination than these minimums and usually provide some additional crime deterrent benefits, but only up to a point.

Other terminology sometimes used is "protective" lighting to indicate that level of illumination that is believed to deter crime, as opposed to that level needed for safety. Lighting used as the sole deterrent to crime has met with some criticism from criminologists. Good lighting is believed to reduce the fear of crime in most people. However, there has been little evidence of a correlation of crime reduction to increased lighting alone.[6]

Most parking lots attached to rental housing properties operate at level one illumination. Level one illumination, if recorded on a light meter, should test around one-half footcandle minimum. A few experts use a less scientific test, such as gauging minimum lighting conditions, for example, by one's ability to read a newspaper or a watch by its illumination. Either test has some value and will determine the level of illumination sufficient for minimum visibility.

Apartment complexes and motel walkways should have illumination minimums in the level two or level three range, depending on the level of crime foreseeability, amount of open space and visibility potential. Residential properties must restrict very bright lighting near sleeping units for obvious reasons. Common area walkways, however, require a level of illumination to allow for recognition of potential danger and should fill in any shadow areas immediately adjacent to those walkways.

A site survey should evaluate the location and effectiveness of light fixtures as well as illumination output. Any burned out light bulbs should be replaced to determine if the fixture is operational. Older apartment buildings are not as likely to have an abundance of exterior light fixtures as a newer building. This is not an inadequacy in properties with low crime foreseeability.

Lighting in the convenience store industry is probably the most critical, followed next by other late night commercial parking facilities. These two facilities have limited options for alternative security measures. Adding personnel is a possibility, but comes with a substantial price tag.

In convenience stores, lighting has proved to be a major consideration in robbery prevention because of high visibility opportunities from the street. The quantity and level of output is important, as well as the balance of illumination in the interior of a store compared to the exterior. If the interior illumination is significantly greater than is the outside illumination, then a mirror effect occurs on the interior windows prohibiting visibility into the parking lot.

Criminals are said to like privacy prior to committing armed robberies. Absence of illumination on the side or rear of a store can sometimes provide that initial privacy. If these conditions exist, they must be considered as part of the overall evaluation.

Aside from certain special applications, lighting has not proved to be a reliable source of crime prevention when there is an absence of natural surveillance opportunities. However, when used in conjunction with good visibility potential and the available personnel to observe, lighting provides an excellent measure of additional protection.

Logically, good visibility and the likelihood of being spotted can be a real deterrent. If no surveillance possibilities exist, the significance of lighting is reduced to a mere condition, which, by our definition, cannot be the sole grounds for foreseeability. A complaint of inadequate lighting would have less probative value if there were no potential to observe the criminal.

Personnel

The use of personnel to provide security is one of the oldest methods of crime prevention. In prehistoric times, cave dwellers probably had someone assigned to watch the entrance to the cave for ferocious animals and other invaders. In modern times, personnel used in the private sector play a role in crime prevention by understanding and implementing policies and procedures, and by observing and reporting discrepancies.

Many premises liability lawsuits alleging inadequate security will focus on the negligence of personnel as the proximate cause of an injury. The process of evaluating personnel for their role in any premises liability litigation involves consideration and review of four important areas.

They are (1) selection criteria, (2) quality of training, (3) supervision, and (4) staffing.

Providing for security by means of personnel does not always mean the application of uniformed security guards. In fact, most security precautions in place in the private sector are supported and maintained by other employees, tenants, and residents of a property. However, because of their popularity in lawsuits, we will discuss the evaluation of the security guard function first.

Security Guards

Traditionally, uniformed guards have been the most visible aspect of a security program designed to secure a premises. They have been utilized for patrol, access control, surveillance, and enforcement of laws and policies.

A common misconception is that uniformed security guards have the training, experience, and powers to arrest similar to police officers.

A second misconception is that uniformed security guards (armed or unarmed) will always interced during a crime and apprehend the perpetrator. Conversely, most security guards are trained only to observe and report crimes and are often specifically directed not to attempt to apprehend an assaillant by their supervisors. One exception might be for those guards who apprehend shoplifters in which they are protecting property, not people. Logically, a security guard cannot observe and report, as expected, if involved in apprehending an assaillant, especially if overpowered or outnumbered.

Records regarding security personnel are normally obtained during the discovery phase. The personnel files of all involved security employees should be requested and reviewed early in the case. Of interest in the file will be their original employment application, performance reviews, letters of commendation or complaint, and other memos and notes.

One of the common issues involving security negligence is the adequacy of the hiring procedures. The entire hiring process should be reviewed and should conform to commonly used methods in the security industry.

These practices may include checking an applicant's background, criminal record, credit history, motor vehicle violations, and references. Jurisdictions will vary on the availability of information. All background information and references should have been rechecked for accuracy, and all credentials such as guard cards, permits, and licenses should have been verified again through the appropriate state of county agencies. Any guard hired to work in a public area should have a command of the English language regardless of the assignment so to be understood by emergency services personnel and witnesses.

Security Guard Training

The next step is to review the training program, if any, provided to each security employee involved. Depending on the experience of the employee and type of property, each security guard should have received, at minimum, a review of all applicable laws governing the procedures for detention and arrest, initial rules and regulations review, on-the-job training, and an opportunity to demonstrate an understanding of all security procedures. Many states require a security guard license or permit, which specifies minimum training periods of one to three days.

A written training manual is desired but not always required. Each employee should have been given a written copy of the company policies and procedures. Manuals should be examined closely for date of policy origin and current effectiveness.

Contract guards assigned to a post should have post orders outlining specific duties and procedures to follow. Complex assignments should have written post orders.

Security Guard Supervision

In larger hotels, apartment complexes, and other properties where security guards and patrols are utilized, it is important to evaluate the level of supervision provided. Many security negligence allegations are proved by demonstrating that necessary security services were either provided in a substandard fashion or not at all. The burden of supervision ultimately belongs to the responsible premises operator. However, the task of supervising the security function is often delegated to a security director or contract guard agency.

Supervision of guards is most commonly accomplished by requiring written activity reports and/or by "clocking in" at prescribed times and locations using an electronic or mechanical device. Evaluation of all written security activity and incident reports for a two year period prior to an incident should be considered standard procedure. These reports are often the best records of the crime activity on a premises. Incomplete or missing reports are often indicative of the effectiveness of the security guard patrol. On the other hand, good documentation of security procedures provide excellent defense exhibits depicting adequate security.

Security Guard Staffing

The amount of security staff necessary to adequately protect a property will vary depending on the size of the property, the nature of the premises, and level of crime foreseeability. Prior staffing levels are usually best obtained from payroll records of the company supplying the security guards. These records should be supplemented by actual schedules showing guard deployment for various days of the week and number of shifts per day.

Security budgets are a third source of staffing records, which can also be helpful in comparing the security expense percentage to the total operational budget. Budget records for several years will indicate whether security expenditures have risen or fallen.

Adequacy of security staffing can be evaluated by schedule review, witness interviews, simulations of actual patrol procedures compared to area of responsibility, and amount of crime still being reported on the property.

Non-security personnel

Aside from security guard personnel, one must evaluate the function and effectiveness of other personnel. In residential properties such as hotels, apartments, and condominiums, Personnel;maintenance staffmaintenance personnel are often the eyes and ears of a property. Resident managers sometimes have the responsibility to patrol the property after hours. These security procedures must be researched in the discovery phase so they can be examined for effectiveness. Housekeeping employees and bellhops can provide visibility and some level of protection from more obvious threats in lodging facilities but are normally not relied upon for protection.

In retail stores, employees are often the only source of security for customers. Convenience stores, for example, are often secured by employees who follow strict cash handling procedures and who supervise the parking lot. In any of these situations, the action or inaction of the employees may be the proximate cause in a premises liability litigation. The basis of liability is again either improper hiring, training, or supervision procedures. Because of this, all emergency plans and written security policies should be obtained and evaluated.

It is not uncommon to find a small retail store, liquor store, or bar operating for years without a single consideration for protecting customers from criminal assault. Many of these small businesses have a long history of criminal activity on the property, which goes unreported to the police. Establishing what were the common security practices, if any, of the business from its employees may be the only source of information available.

Violation of company policies and established common practices can often be important factors in evaluating the adequacy of security allegations involving personnel.

Oftentimes, negligence has been proven by showing gross or intentional violations of company policy, especially if those policies involved serious customer safety issues.

Written security policies should be verified against actual daily activity records for compliance with those policies.

Breach of Contract

A common misconception in premises liability litigation is that a contact security guard company, hired to provide security on a property, owes the same legal duty of protection to a plaintiff as does a land owner. Usually, contract guard companies have only to fulfill the terms of its contract by performing their duties in a reasonable manner (substantial performance).

Except by specific agreement, security guard duties generally are to observe, report, and act as a visual deterrent, but not necessarily to prevent or interced in a physical altercation. An exception might be when a security guard promises or assures protection to a person and fails to do so. Otherwise, no legal duty of protection usually is owed to a land entrant other than performing reasonably.

The theory of liability necessary to prevail against a contract guard company is one of negligence or from an intentional act on the part of a guard that directly caused an injury. Either act will usually be sufficient evidence to prove a breach of contract, and therefore potential exposure for the landowner and guard company.

Procedures

Policies and procedures are often not viewed as true security methods, yet few security programs could be implemented without sound policies and procedures. Since procedures are the means by which hardware, personnel, and facility design features are integrated, they are the foundation of an effective security plan.

Procedures generally take the form of a written training manual in larger companies and directives or memos in smaller ones. Regardless of the type of security method, procedures are required to establish the plan for implementing, utilizing, and maintaining the security controls.

Procedures are often involved in premises liability litigation issues. Security policies and procedures, when first written up in a policy manual, usually represent the highest intentions in service and protection. Security policies and procedures, for our purposes, would include a method for maintaining existing hardware as well as for directing personnel.

Security procedures have a tendency to weaken in time unless rigidly supervised. In times of low profitability, businesses will sometimes cut out certain security duties, especially if extra employees or equipment are required to maintain the procedure. A worse case scenario is when proven security programs are eliminated because the past threat has been temporarily reduced. Whatever the reason for the cut, the original security policy manual rarely gets updated. In a premises liability litigation, out-of-date policy and procedure manuals are the kiss of death at trial.

In an apartment rape case where door locking hardware failed or is alleged to be defective, all maintenance records for that particular unit become relevant, as do any records of failure to repair in a timely manner. The procedures for notification of a defect of a security precaution and the timeliness of its ultimate repair will be evaluated.

Key Control

Procedures for controlling room keys and master keys are relevant to evaluate in lodging facilities and apartment complexes when an assailant allegedly gains entry by key. Records of lock core and key changes are important to obtain and review. Evidence of control of all levels of master keys by number or code is required. Except for newer magnetically coded access card systems, every key control system requires written records to maintain control over distribution. If no records are available, it may be reasonable to infer that no system exists. A good procedure for apartment door locks would be to change locks, at minimum, whenever a key is reported missing or a tenant moves out.

Testing of Procedures

Procedures are commonly written to support hardware and equipment. A system for locking certain doors and for turning on exterior lighting and alarm systems is relevant if the failure to do so is the alleged proximate cause to an assault.

Sometimes simulations are required to test the adequacy of certain procedures in light of their potential for exposure. An adequate procedure may require a backup procedure or double check to be deemed sufficient. For example, a procedure of watching customers enter a parking structure via video camera may not be adequate if communication and reponse potential are not available.

Conclusion

The evaluation of physical security measures of a premises must be conducted by a qualified security expert as soon as possible following an incident. The site survey should be examined for the four areas of security methodology to assure a complete evaluation.

Simulations and tests should be conducted anytime a defective condition is alleged or uncertainty in the testimony exists, and documentation, including photographs, should be obtained.

Photographs should be taken to capture the physical design and other attributes on record. The effectiveness of certain policies and procedures should be tested, if possible, while on site to evaluate them for effectiveness.

Endnotes

1. *Webster's Ninth New Collegiate Dictionary*, *s. v.* "deter," and "prevent."
2. Philip Jenkins, *Crime and Justice, Issues and Ideas* (Monterey, Calif.: Brooks/Cole Publishing Company, 1984), 152.
3. Thomas Gabor, "The Crime Displacement Hypothesis: An Empirical Examination," *Crime & Delinquency* (July, 1981), 390-404.
4. International Conference of Building Officials, *Uniform Building Security Code* (Whittier, Calif.: I. C. B. O., 1979).
5. Illuminating Engineering Society of North America, *IES Lighting Handbook* (New York: IES Publications, published annually). See also other IES publications for more detailed information.
6. James M. Tien, *et al.*, *Street Lighting Projects* (Washington D. C.: U. S. Department of Justice, Law Enforcement Assis-

tance Administration, National Institute of Law Enforcement and Criminal Justice, 1979).

CHAPTER TEN

Testing and Research

Often overlooked in premises liability matters are the negligence issues arising from non-compliance with local codes and ordinances.

Complaints of inadequate security are commonly due to alleged defects in door and window locks and defective lighting. This is especially true with rental housing, hotels and motels, and apartment complexes.

Inadequate locking hardware may be due to violation of building codes or ordinances, tending to prove negligence *per se* and breach of duty. In this case, the alleged breach of duty stems from an implied warranty of habitability and from failure to use ordinary care.

Similarly, substandard door hardware could be viewed as a defective condition, if that hardware was not code quality and failed to function as expected.

Research for Codes and Ordinances

By contacting the city or county, usually the planning department, one can obtain much of the necessary information regarding proper zoning, building and security codes, fire codes, building permit requirements, and other ordinances. This information is a matter of public record and can be accessed by anyone.

Zoning

Most metropolitan areas have strict zoning requirements. Zoning usually comes under the jurisdiction of a city planning department, whose basic function is to plan and regulate land use within a city, so that industrial, commercial and residential areas are not in conflict. Zoning maps are readily available to the public.

In a premises liability litigation, zoning may become an issue, for example, when a residential property owner decides to remodel a garage into an apartment and rent it out for extra income. Zoning may prohibit a change in land use to multi-residential property. Failure to obtain a zoning variance often sets up a pattern of avoiding building permits and other inspections. City services, police, and fire departments may be unaware of changes and of the new tenants.

Building Permits

Building permits are generally required for construction of a new structure or when remodeling an existing one. The permit system is designed to allow for an inspection process by which a qualified person will approve plans, quality of workmanship, and compliance to code standards.

Since hiring licensed building contractors is not mandatory, these inspections are an important step in insuring quality of workmanship by non-licensed workers.

Any new or recently remodeled structure involved in a premises liability litigation should have its file researched for permits approved and signed off by qualified inspectors. Building permit files are normally available through the city or county building inspector's office.

Building Codes

The Uniform Building Code was first published in 1927 by the International Conference of Building Officials,[1] providing a code that could be formally adopted and utilized by state and local government. Jurisdiction's may have additional regulations or amendments to their code, and each should be researched individually.

Although some older buildings may not be affected by current codes, new and remodeled structures must comply with present standards of construction. Construction and material compliance to code can sometimes make the difference between an assailant gaining access or not.

Uniform Building Security Code

Building codes do not directly address security issues unless the Uniform Building Security Code, Chapter 41 of the Uniform Building Code, is locally adopted. The Uniform Building Security Code was first published in 1979 by the International Conference of Building Officials, establishing minimum standards for making dwellings resistant to unlawful entry. This security code pins down many variables involved in the type, use, and age of a building by providing exact standards of materials and testing.

The code:

> regulates swinging doors, sliding doors, windows, and hardware in connection with dwelling units of apartment houses or one- and two-family dwellings. The level of resistance to unlawful entry established by standards in this code is directed at the novice burglar. The code gives consideration to the concerns of police, fire, and building officials in establishing requirements for resistance to burglary which is compatible with fire and life safety.[2]

Adoption of the Uniform Building Security Code should be researched at the state and local level in any litigation involving a rental property built or remodeled since 1979. If adopted by a jurisdiction, the structure can be evaluated using the code as the minimum standard of care.

A common scenario might include a home owner who decides to remodel a large house into four rental apartments. To save money, the work is completed by casual labor and without proper permits. The result is poor quality door and window locking hardware not meeting the Uniform Building Security Code code requirements. An assailant enters one of the units by slipping the substandard door lock and assaults the tenant. Litigation could prove costly for this landlord based on a clear violation of codes caused by circumventing building permits and by demonstrating a profit motive over tenant safety.

Local Ordinances

Ordinances are adopted and enforced by a local jurisdiction for a specific purpose. To resolve rising crime problems, a jurisdiction may decide to create an ordinance by adopting the Uniform Building Security Code or by modifying it. Certain industries are affected by ordinances more than others.

Some cities have strict security regulations for commercial businesses or rental housing properties, which specify exact standards for security equipment and procedures. Convenience stores, for example, in some cities are controlled by ordinances that specify hours of operation, number of staff on duty, and requirements for special robbery prevention training for employees.

In 1963, the City of Oakland, (California) passed an ordinance[3] requiring all unattended commercial buildings to have physical security measures installed to prevent unauthorized entry. The ordinance has minimum standards in door and window security hardware and requires additional alarm systems in some cases.

In Akron, Ohio, in 1981, the city enacted a "Late Night Sales Ordinance"[4] to provide security measures between the hours of 12 midnight and 6 am for retail establishments and gasoline stations. This ordinance specifies robbery prevention measures to include employee robbery prevention training, use of a drop safe, anti-robbery signage, unobstructed windows, and minimum lighting standards.

In Florida, the city of Gainesville approved an ordinance in 1986[5] that required late night convenience stores to employ a minimum of two employees between the hours of 8:00 pm and 4:00 am, installation of security precautions such as a timed-access drop safe, video camera, minimum light standards, cash handling policy, unobstructed windows, and anti-robbery signs, and to implement robbery prevention training for all employees. Non-compliance with these minimum standards are sometimes viewed as negligence *per se*.

Simulations

Frequently, when a defective policy or procedure is alleged, it becomes necessary to conduct a simulation to verify the defect. In other cases, it is probative to conduct a simulation to validate or invalidate certain facts alleged in witness testimony. These simulations should be conducted by a qualified person who will be capable of testifying in court if necessary.

Factual simulations are easiest to recreate when the conditions are similar to the actual event. For example, a security guard reported observing a defendant's employee walking down an exterior staircase from the fourth level of a parking garage, moments after an assault had occurred. In later deposition testimony, the guard marked precisely on a diagram the exact spot of the guard post. A simulation was conducted duplicating the positions of both the security guard post and subject staircase. This procedure found that a roof overhang made it impossible for the guard to see either the suspect or the staircase. Subsequent cross-examination revealed that the security guard had merely assumed that the suspect had descended the staircase.

Simulations require prior research to identify the conditions that existed on the day of the incident involved in the litigation.

Relevant conditions might be: the weather, including cloud cover and temperature; the time of sun/moon rise or set; the angle of the sun; and the phase of the moon. This research may prove critical in litigation where lighting levels are in dispute, or the extent of visibility is an issue.

For example, a plaintiff claimed to have been the victim of an assault where a suspect had the plaintiff at knife point inside a parking garage. A security guard walked within one hundred feet and appeared to look directly at the plaintiff. The security guard claimed that no activity was observed. Research determined that the lighting conditions were inadequate to allow identification of persons at that distance. A simulation using similar subjects proved that identification of an assailant or a knife at that distance would have been impossible due to the shadows and visual obstructions inside the garage.

Only established authorities, such as the United States Naval Observatory almanac tables[6] should be used for sunrise and sunset times. This source, and others, are highly reliable and usually admissible by the court. Weather information should be obtained in writing from local meteorologists who file daily reports with the newspapers and television networks.

Simulations are always recommended if the adequacy of guard patrols is at issue. Time and distance studies that demonstrate the amount of time required to completely patrol a complex have proved to be relevant in cases where guard deployment is at issue.

For example, security guard activity reports for an airport parking lot consistently recorded six complete walking tours of the lot within an eight hour shift, including lunch and breaks. During a simulation, one complete tour of the lot took over three hours. The mathematics of the time and distance simulation did not match the guard reports. The airport client was neither well served nor correctly informed of the actual coverage by the guard company.

In another case, a contract guard service was to drive completely through an apartment complex parking lot every two hours in a marked security vehicle and conduct a walk-through of the entire grounds as well. This guard patrol also monitored another property several miles away. A plaintiff who had been assaulted claimed that the patrol could not have possibly serviced both sites adequately. The guard company submitted daily activity reports showing compliance with this contract. A simulation of the driving and walking procedure took forty minutes for each tour, assuming no problems were discovered, and took five minutes to drive between sites. Time cards and billing records produced by the contract guard company supported that same time allocation per day. The coverage was very thorough and was said to have produced a "ghost effect," where most tenants believed there to be several guards on patrol each night due to the combination of vehicle and foot patrol. The defendant subsequently prevailed.

Testing

Tests and verification of certain physical aspects of a premises are frequently necessary when a hardware defect is alleged to be the proximate cause of an assault. Other than highly sophisticated testing, most tests can be conducted by a security expert during a site survey. Doors and windows can be subjected to basic hand manipulation testing. Sliding glass doors and windows can be tested to see if they can be lifted out of the track or forced open with average hand and tool manipulation. Entry doors can be tested for the general strength of construction as well as for suitability and condition of locks, strike plates, and door frames.

Accurate measurements are sometimes required to prove or disprove statements made by witnesses. For example, an elderly witness claimed to have been within fifty feet of an apartment owner's employee and to have seen that person open a secured door with a key and assault a tenant. Measurements taken using landmarks provided by the witness demonstrated the actual distance to be over two hundred feet and the actual time was to be dusk, making recognition of an assailant extremely remote.

Illumination Testing

Inadequate lighting levels are commonly alleged in premises liability complaints. Preliminary testing for adequacy of lighting can be conducted by an experienced security expert. For more complex readings, professional lighting engineers can be retained to test illumination levels using sophisticated light meters. Qualified practitioners can be located through the Illuminating Engineering Society.[7]

There is disagreement among consultants on the standards required for accurate testing of illumination, and whether to specify footcandle minimums or other visibility criteria (e.g., being able to read a newspaper or your watch). Footcandles or lumens provide little information to lay jurors, so exact scientific illumination output measurements are not always informative.

Most jurors will understand whether lighting is adequate using common terms, regardless of the exact measurement. Keep in mind that, as defined, lighting levels are mere conditions at a particular time and location at a site.

Hardware Testing

Tests of hardware or equipment sometimes may require the services of a professional testing lab. Most equipment and hardware used in the security industry have testing criteria developed either by the federal government, a testing agency, or a manufacturer. These criteria have been disputed by some specialists but for the most part are an excellent reference point from which to gauge adequacy.

Equipment tests are necessary when a defect is alleged, or security hardware is believed to be substandard. An example would be a sliding glass door in a condominium unit where an assailant gained entry. Precise testing standards are available, which can be applied to the door to test its suitability for preventing intrusion.[8] These standards are available for doors, door frames, door locks, dead bolts, windows, and sliding glass doors.

These complex tests should be conducted only by qualified engineers with the proper test equipment and previous experience. A security expert familiar with these standards can perform preliminary tests and provide an early indication of whether a particular piece of hardware is likely to pass or fail the actual test.

Photography

All tests and simulations should be supported by photographs to add extra credibility to the activity. Visual reference points are an important aid in understanding the significance of the test or simulation. Photographs also document the existence of important evidence and make excellent exhibits in court.

An experienced photographer using good equipment will produce the desired results more often than an amateur with an "instamatic." If the quality of the photography is important, consider using a forensic photographer. A forensic photographer is trained to capture the best photographic record possible for use in court and is experienced in the use of macro-lenses and can provide precise close-up shots. The subject will usually be properly framed, while shadow and highlights remain sharp when enlarged for court display.

Color print film should be used whenever the shot duplicates what the human eye would see. Black and white film prints are often better for close-up work, low light situations, or when detail is more important than color.

All photographs need to be labeled in some manner soon after being printed to assure accuracy, with adhesive labels for the back of each photograph, or "post-it" type notes for the front side to identify particular objects in the shot. Use of an electronic "data-back" device on the camera to superimpose the date or time onto the film negative adds credibility when the time factor is at issue.

Conclusion

Research of codes and ordinances can be an important first step in a litigation, particularly involving rental housing or convenience stores. Checking compliance with codes and ordinances is effective for either plaintiff or defendant in dealing with minimum standard of care questions.

Testing and simulations can provide important evidence, which will have a high degree of credibility if shown to be objective and accurate. These procedures should be conducted early in a litigation in order to duplicate the conditions of an incident.

Professional photographs are an excellent way to provide visual aids and documentation of important evidence and testing procedures.

ENDNOTES

1. International Conference of Building Officials, *Uniform Building Code* (Whittier, Calif.: I. C. B. O.) Published every three years.
2. International Conference of Building Officials, *Uniform Building Security Code* (Whittier, Calif.: I. C. B. O., 1979), 5. Published every three years.
3. City of Oakland, California, "Oakland Burglary Security Ordinance," Ordinance No. 6899 C. M. S., Municipal Code, Article 12, Sections 3-12.08 - 3-12.20, 1963.
4. City of Akron, Ohio, "Late Night Sales," Chapter 660, Section 660.10, *Codified Ordinances of the City of Akron,* 1981.
5. City of Gainesville, Florida, Ordinance No. 3230-0-86-30, 1986.
6. Nautical Almanac Office, United States Naval Observatory, "Sunset and Sunrise Tables," (Washington, D.C.: U.S. Government Printing Office, 1965).
7. Illuminating Engineering Society of North America, 345 East 47th Street, New York, NY, 10017.
8. American Society for Testing and Materials, 1916 Race Street, Philadelphia, PA, 19103-1187.

TRIAL PREPARATION

CHAPTER ELEVEN

The Discovery Phase

Opposing attorneys have the opportunity to identify and exchange necessary information and documents in the discovery phase before trial. This period generates a tremendous volume of legal documents.

The discovery phase may be the most confusing time for defendant property owners. Many property owners have stated that this process of being required to produce files and records to a plaintiff is a traumatic experience. Many security departments have been torn apart under the scrutiny of a plaintiff inquiry. Under the microscope of a litigation investigation, all the flaws, errors, bad decisions, and personnel problems of a security program are subject to examination.

The purpose of this chapter is to discuss some of the critical aspects of the discovery phase as they affect a premises liability litigation. Since more than ninety percent of all premises liability cases are disposed of before trial, this phase will often determine the amount of settlement, if any.

This chapter is directed primarily at trial attorneys. However, it should also be of benefit to security professionals and property owners. By understanding the process of discovery, one can alleviate some of the fear of the litigation process. In addition, a business owner or operator will learn the importance of maintaining a viable security system, documentation, and other records necessary to defend this type of lawsuit.

Liability Issues

Before the information gathering process can start, both plaintiff and defense lawyers must research the existing case law and develop their theories of liability. All parties must develop a clear understanding of the applicable issues such as legal duty, crime foreseeability, and adequacy of security early in a litigation if they are to maximize the case potential.

Most attorneys have never accepted a premises liability case where crime foreseeability and adequacy of security were the primary issues. The ability to identify all potential liability issues, formulate the type of discovery strategy likely to produce the desired information, is a difficult task without expert assistance. Assistance from an expert soon after a lawsuit is filed will provide a distinct advantage in the preparation of a case. In too many cases security experts are not consulted until after the discovery period is closed and witnesses are no longer available.

Discovery Components

There are three primary components of the discovery phase that will be discussed in this chapter: (1) interrogatories, (2) production of documents, including physical evidence, and (3) depositions.

Our intention is to comment only on the important aspects of each component as it relates to the security issues of a premises liability evaluation, and on how each phase might be used to maximum potential.

Relevant to all three components is a time decay factor. Information must be obtained as soon as possible following an incident to increase accuracy and the probability of obtaining records.

In the Appendix is a sample discovery list suitable for a parking lot assault case at a shopping center.

Interrogatories

During the discovery phase, parties will request much of the information necessary for litigation directly from opposing counsel in the form of written interrogatory questions. Among other things, interrogatories are normally propounded to identify entities, witnesses, and certain documents.

The first set of interrogatories should be developed and sent as soon as possible to allow for maximum response potential. As discussed above, witnesses, data and documentation have a "shelf life," whereafter documents and witness memories will begin to fade away. Company buy-outs and management changes have disrupted and caused the premature settlement of more than one defensible case due to lost witnesses and records.

Knowledgeable attorneys who propound interrogatory questions tailored specifically for the case being litigated will send a message to opposing counsel that they mean business. Standard form interrogatories often are unproductive because they send a message of inattention to the issues of the case and allow opposing counsel the opportunity to submit nonresponsive answers.

Identity of the Parties

It is extremely important to identify all entities involved and their business relationships. On more than one occasion, attorneys have filed suit against the wrong parties or failed to identify and name all the entities who should be involved in the litigation. By the time the error was realized, the statute of limitations had run, severely affecting the outcome of the case. Defendants sometimes are forced to file a cross-complaint if other, more responsible entities responsible have not been named by a plaintiff.

Security Issues

Aside from the standard interrogatories, certain questions should be reserved to identify specifically the security issues involved. There are very specific relationships, titles, documents, and materials that are commonly used in the security profession. In security negligence cases, for example, the identity of all security personnel files, training manuals, time cards, deployment schedules, and activity reports would be of prime concern to a plaintiff. The name of the custodian of records and precise title of each record should be requested in an effort to produce the desired documents later.

A defendant in a premises liability litigation may already be aware of the nature of the incident. Despite this, the defense attorney must formulate questions for the plaintiff to determine the nature of the allegation, and the extent of injuries claimed, to be able to refute the allegation. Defense attorneys also have the task of responding to the plaintiff's interrogatories and request for production of documents.

Because of various legal tactics, interrogatory questions are often returned with nonresponsive answers (e.g., vague and ambiguous, unable to locate, unknown). This tactic sometimes will work against attorneys who are on tight timetables, or who are not willing to resubmit more precise questions. Although some jurisdictions limit the number of interrogatories, submitting additional, more precise questions is likely to produce the desired information. Interrogatory answers can be of benefit, even when the desired documents are said to be nonexistent. This essentially prohibits the opposing counsel from using the same information later.

In the Appendix, we have listed sample interrogatory "theme" questions, appropriate for a shopping center matter. These questions should be of interest to all parties and useful for case preparation.

Document Production

Interrogatory answers and initial witness interviews often provide the necessary information required to allow for this step in case development. Opposing attorneys will submit a formal request for production of documents in an effort to obtain records held by the other side.

The review of documents regarding the operation of a premises is a major and critical component in developing an opinion on the adequacy of security issues. Of greatest importance are written policies and procedures, in-house security records, staffing schedules, maintenance records, lease agreements, budgets, and other operational documents. These records are the key to evaluating the issues and how operational policies and procedures may have impacted crime potential. This information usually can not be obtained from any source other than the defendant.

Depending on the ability and experience of an attorney, document production can be either a productive or a costly exercise. The approach of asking the opposing counsel for every document that exists and then sifting through the pile hoping for enlightenment does not seem logical nor effective. For example, contract security guards usually complete daily activity reports and incident reports.

Security dispatchers usually keep a dispatch log by date and time of all calls from the field. Specific reference to these particular documents will get the attention of opposing counsel. On the other hand, uninspiring discovery attempts by plaintiffs often send a message that they are still fishing for liability. This frequently results in a delay and inhibits early settlement offers.

The presence or absence of supporting documentation will often make the difference in credibility of the security program being evaluated. An established shopping center, for example, should be expected to have a security guard training program, written daily reports, and a level of staffing to allow for adequate deployment of the guards. The documentation produced should contain all of the above information and more if an affirmative defense is planned. Lack of evidence or documentation of a shopping center security program will be difficult to overcome in an industry that traditionally uses guards.

Review of documentation by a security expert can provide additional theories of liability which should be analyzed and developed into a defense strategy. After reviewing the materials, additional questions should be raised by the expert. Those questions should be discussed to evaluate what effect they may have on the present case. This may cause the generation of a second list requesting more documents to be produced.

Physical Evidence

Another area frequently overlooked is physical evidence obtained from the crime scene, often used as an exhibit at the criminal trial. Examples are the knife used by an assailant in a parking lot fight, the ladder left unattended by painters and found under an apartment window of a rape victim, and the screwdriver used to lift out a sliding glass window in a homicide victim's condominium.

Physical evidence such as a gun, club, or tool cannot always be released by the police. However, these items can be examined under their supervision and photographed at the police station.

Such items can be of great benefit as visual aids, and can be offered as proof to support other testimony. For example, in a convenience store case, the store owner claimed that the baseball bat used by a clerk to bludgeon a thief belonged to his son's baseball team. The bat, obtained and produced for trial, had the word "Equalizer" painted on it, along with notches carved in the handle from previous usage. Needless to say, the case settled immediately.

Photographs, audio recordings, and videotapes are generally taken by the police during the course of any serious assaultive crime investigation. Copies are obtainable by way of subpoena in most jurisdictions, if sentence has already been passed. These photographs and tapes may depict the actual conditions of an assault site. Premises liability lawsuits have been both won and lost based on police photographs and tapes.

As an example, a police photograph may resolve conflicting testimony about whether a dead bolt lock was in place or determine if a sliding glass door was open or closed. A security camera videotape depicting a department store robbery may clearly show the chain of events and the negligent act of the security guard in attempting to subdue the robbers, leading to the injury of a plaintiff.

As with every other piece of information discussed, physical evidence will eventually disappear. Many police agencies destroy evidence on an annual basis once the criminal phase is completed. These items or their images should be obtained during the discovery phase.

Depositions

Lay persons often do not understand the purpose or importance of a deposition. For this reason, we will review the basic points here.

More than one competent attorney has said that the deposition phase is really a test run of a trial. The fact that over ninety percent of all litigation cases never go to trial seems to support that belief.

Depositions are sometimes the only opportunity for extracting testimony from the opposing parties and witnesses before trial. Depositions are useful for expanding upon initial statements of witnesses and hopefully pinning down their testimony.

Depositions also provide an opportunity to question any opposing experts regarding their opinions and proposed courtroom testimony. For the above reasons and more, preparing thoroughly for each deposition is highly recommended.

The law enforcement and security records, the field interviews, the code and ordinance research, the tests and simulations, the interrogatory answers, and the documents produced by opposing counsel should provide a direction for questions to be asked in depositions. With this information in hand, it becomes much easier to formulate thoughtful questions designed to draw out the desired response.

Most witness depositions represent individual factual testimony and are normally limited accordingly. One of the most overlooked areas in deposing witnesses is personal identifier questions. In order to locate a witness several years after the fact, one must obtain personal information such as maiden name, date of birth, social security number, name and address of parents, and employment histories.

Asking about future relocation plans is also helpful if the witness is critical to a litigation. The witness will usually supply permanent contact persons for future reference.

Consulting with a security expert for assistance in developing deposition "theme" questions is highly recommended. Questions can be formulated to probe or develop the security issues involved. Precise questioning can positively affect the outcome of a case.

Depositions of present and former security employees of a defendant business can be crucial to a premises liability litigation.

Using a Security Expert

Security experts are utilized in this type of lawsuit to evaluate the security issues and render an opinion to a jury. Experts are required in most jurisdictions when the liability issues before the court are outside of the common experience of the lay jury. An expert must be objective regarding these issues to be viewed as credible by the jury.

Important cases have been both won and lost based on the decision to consult a security expert. Retain the best expert available early, and then consult with that expert as necessary throughout the preparation of a case.

Generally, an expert will obtain factual witness information by reviewing copies of all relevant documents and depositions. For expense control purposes, some attorneys send excerpts or summaries of transcripts involving the security issues. This method is not recommended. Not disclosing entire witness testimony to an expert could prove to be disastrous at their deposition or during trial.

Ask the expert to make page-line summaries of any relevant issues. These notes should be reviewed with the attorney at the first opportunity. A security expert will always read and interpret testimony differently than an attorney and will probably have a list of questions to discuss. Do not be concerned regarding these deposition summaries being in an expert's file. As long as they are summaries of longer, discoverable documents, they are necessary and certainly not privileged.

Security experts can also be effectively used by asking them to draft a declaration for use during a motion in support or opposition of summary judgment or for an arbitration. This preliminary opportunity is often overlooked.

Expert declarations can be persuasive and provide that extra edge necessary to prove your argument.

The Expert's Deposition

A security expert's deposition represents an overview of the entire case. Expert opinion testimony can be based on a broad range of testimony and evidence. An expert's opinion testimony is more liberally allowed by most judges and is often the highpoint of the case. An uninspired deposition of an expert can prove disastrous later on in trial.

A security expert needs to consider the testimony of all factual witnesses as well as other relevant expert witnesses. For this reason, the deposition of a security expert should be scheduled last or near last. Exceptions would be for medical or economic experts dealing primarily with the damage issues.

The importance of reviewing the opinions and theories of one's own security expert prior to their deposition should be obvious. It is surprising, however, to learn how many experts express their opinions for the first time to the retaining attorney just moments before their deposition. It is also fairly common to have an inexperienced expert blurt out personal opinions in testimony not previously discussed with the attorney. Practice with your expert will eliminate most surprises and will sharpen the skills necessary to challenge the opposing expert effectively.

Preparation for deposing an opposing security expert should involve extra time and effort. It is essential that expert's have had time to read, research, and survey everything necessary for them to develop a complete opinion regarding the issues prior to being deposed. Premature depositions are usually unproductive, while losing the strategic advantage of the first encounter.

It is common practice for a security expert to assist in developing deposition questions for the opposing expert. An expert should know how to challenge the opinions and theories of other experts by developing hypotheticals designed to pin down even the most experienced practitioners. This is especially helpful when the opinions expressed by the opposing expert are unreasonable or unsound.

In the Appendix are sample "theme" questions for use in *voir dire* (qualification) of a security expert.

Prior to deposition, an expert should prepare a current resume to be used for *voir dire* purposes. It should include qualification information such as work experience, formal education, security training, licenses and certifications, and activities in the security industry.

Next, an expert should develop a list of every document reviewed, every witness contacted, and all research and tests conducted in preparation for opinion testimony. All documents, notes, and reports, not subject to privilege, should be available for production at the time of deposition.

Jurisdictions and rules will vary; however, following the above procedure will reduce the chance of testimony being excluded later in trial.

Written opinions of a security expert are rarely requested by either party. One exception is usually in the case of a written declaration by an expert to support or oppose a motion to the court for summary judgment or for other administrative proceedings.

Conclusion

The discovery phase is a critical period where much information is exchanged by the involved parties. The attorney who focuses on the liability issues early and immediately starts to locate documents, witnesses and other information will have the advantage at trial or settlement conferences. Obtaining records and physical evidence before they disappear is a basic, but often overlooked, responsibility.

Preparing one's own expert sufficiently in advance should also prepare one to properly question the opinions and qualifications of the opposing expert. Experts should be used to assist, if necessary, as a sounding board in presenting and attacking opinions on liability issues.

CHAPTER TWELVE

Effective Trial Presentation

A premises liability litigation set for trial usually means all efforts for settlement between the parties have failed. In most cases, a jury will now hear the case and decide who shall prevail. A plaintiff is gambling on a jury verdict and an award higher than previously offered, while the defense is betting on a defense verdict or reduced award. In tightly contested litigation with many disputed facts, the outcome is often determined by which side is better prepared and more persuasive.

Security issues in a premises liability case are usually complex. The concept of legal duty and crime foreseeability are confusing for most trial attorneys, and even more confusing for a lay jury.

Important facts presented over the course of a two week trial can be hopelessly forgotten in the parade of witnesses and legal arguments. Because of this, it is critical to prepare a clear, well organized, presentation of the security issues.

Presentation of Security Issues

Using this book as a guide, each component of litigation can be discussed in some detail to a jury. By breaking down the complex legal issues into component parts, most jurors will understand the necessary criteria to guide their decision. Once explained to a jury, the liability issues will make sense when reassembled into a whole "cause of action" or defense strategy.

The phrase, "educating the jury," is accurate. Jurors must be given a crash course in security and liability in the time frame of a trial. The topics necessary for presentation to a jury are incorporated into the chapter headings of this book. The method of presentation is a matter of personal style. Basically, it is essential to reiterate each point and summarize clearly.

Elements of the Tort

For any premises liability litigation to be deemed successful, it must be legally sound and survive the scrutiny of an appellate review. It is important then to clearly establish that all the elements of the tort are present and then proceed to either prove or disprove the allegations.

As a review, the five basic components are as follows: (1) the land possessor owed a legal duty of care to the plaintiff; (2) the land possessor knew that assaultive crime was reasonably foreseeable on the premises; (3) the owner failed (negligence) to exercise a reasonable standard of care (protection); (4) that negligence was the proximate cause of the plaintiff's assault; and (5) the plaintiff was damaged (injured) as a result of that breach of duty.

An effective presentation to a jury might include an explanation of each element involved.

The Concept of Duty

Jurors need to be told about the issue of legal duty. Often, jurors will have different personal views on whether a business or property owner is supposed to provide security. Many people believe that once customer's go into the parking lot, the merchant no longer has responsibility to protect them from harm. On the other hand, jurors also need to understand that a legal duty can be satisfied by the land possessor by providing a reasonable amount of security, regardless of the seriousness of any resulting injuries to a plaintiff.

Research will be conducted by attorneys in their own jurisdiction to establish what the case law dictates regarding legal duty before presenting these arguments to a jury. Even though legal duty is a matter of law, not fact, a juror's understanding of the concept will aid in the deliberation of the remaining elements. The court will rule, generally, one way or the other on the issue of legal duty before a trial begins, and deliberation instructions will be given to a jury by the judge.

Knowledge of Crime Foreseeability

The concept of crime foreseeability is the most difficult aspect to understand of all the tort elements. A synopsis of the five chapters in this book on crime foreseeability would provide a jurors with a complete information base and allow them to make a more informed decision because of that training.

It is important for a jury to understand the nature of a premises as discussed in Chapter Five. Most jurors will understand the probability of future crime issues better when they can apply it to a particular property type. Whether the property is open to the public, semiprivate or caters to young people will affect the weight of evidence presented.

Crime demographic evidence is often in dispute: which types of crime are relevant, for what time period, and for what distance from a property should they be admissible? Previous crime activity can be very damaging if presented clearly and accurately. On the other hand, lack of crime history can be an important defense strategy.

Great care should be exercised when gathering and preparing statistical data. Attempts to over-manipulate the statistics can destroy the credibility of the presenting witness. Errors will also destroy the credibility of the crime data.

Visual Aids

Visual aids such as aerial photos, charts, or graphs displaying crime demographics of a particular site and surrounding area will dramatically increase the comprehension of jurors. It is recommended that all motions limiting the admissibility of crime statistics be addressed prior to preparing expensive charts. Courtroom exhibits that are inaccurate or contain even one excluded piece of evidence will generally not be admissible in court.

Color should be used for all exhibits instead of black and white, if applicable, and be legible at fifteen feet. The exhibit should be clear and uncluttered to obtain maximum understanding. Professional looking charts are often viewed as more credible because they are easier to understand.

The goal of the presentation on crime foreseeability is to establish the "level" of crime potential as being either (1) not foreseeable, (2) low, (3) moderate, or (4) high.

Because this level is likely to be disputed by the opposing counsel, the jury will have to decide based on the presentations of both parties.

Once established, this level of crime foreseeability will be used as a gauge for the jury to evaluate the adequacy of security precautions on the defendant's property.

Presentation on Adequacy

The third provable element of this particular tort litigation involves the issues of adequacy of security. As explained in Chapters Eight and Nine, the definitions of the words adequacy and security can be misleading. Although they are difficult concepts, they can be explained more easily than crime foreseeability.

A common trap for many attorneys is to assume that jurors know the difference between the effectiveness of one security measure versus another. On the contrary, surveys have shown that jurors' opinions differ depending on their background and what they have been told or have seen in the media. Because of this problem, it is important to align the jury's thinking by making a sound presentation on the definition of the term adequate.

A presentation to a jury on the definition of reasonableness and standard of care is also necessary to provide them with a gauge by which to evaluate. This presentation is extremely important to defendants who have provided for security in some manner. It needs to be reiterated that security is not required to be perfect or omnipresent. On the other hand, the same presentation can show how a particular landlord failed to measure up to the reasonable standard of care of the industry or of the community.

At trial, security experts retained by each side usually have differing and sometimes opposing opinions on the adequacy of security issues, but both cannot be right. The jury will have to decide once again.

The value of a proper presentation to the jury becomes obvious. An educated juror will be better able to understand, analyze, and interpret the data. A professional security expert will have an advantage in this area by being able to provide practical examples, showing how one security measure is more adequate and practical than another in a common application. The security expert who facilitates that presentation, if sound, will often be seen as more credible than one who merely renders an opinion.

Presentation on Security

A finding of adequate security is not the result of the evaluation of a single security device or piece of hardware, but rather an evaluation of whether a combination of security measures in place was reasonably adequate to prevent or deter reasonably foreseeable crimes. The fact that a plaintiff was injured should not be an automatic condemnation of any particular security measure or combination of measures.

Unfortunately, many cases have been won or lost based solely on whether a particular security device was in place and functioning. Chapter Nine outlined a method for examining any security program, including a detailed explanation of security methodology and how it is commonly applied.

A presentation to a jury should include a review of these methods commonly used to provide for security. Each industry has specific common practices used to address certain security issues. These common practices can be used, instead of strict standards, as a guide for evaluating security adequacy.

When applicable, codes and ordinances should be presented as minimum standards by which a property owner should have been in compliance. This presentation will educate jurors and provide the criteria from which they can make an informed decision.

Adequacy of security is conceptually connected to the level of crime foreseeability already established. Reasonable security should be that amount that is designed to prevent or deter future foreseeable crimes. It does not have to be perfect or provide higher than necessary levels of protection.

Photographs and Scale Drawings

Photographs and scale drawings are extremely important to provide graphic support for expert testimony. Close-up or macro-photography of a lock or other security device can be important demonstrative evidence depicting either a functional or defective condition. Scale drawings can be used to illustrate distances, obstacles, and the location of security devices. Photographs and drawings are helpful because they allow visualization of the subject matter. They can be used for corroboration of certain facts, tests or simulations.

A major benefit is that these exhibits will be placed in the jury room during deliberation and can be viewed many times, while witness testimony is heard only once.

Negligence

The issue of whether a defendant was negligent is for a jury to decide. A presentation to a jury needs to include a discussion on how to decide if a land possessor was negligent for failure to provide adequate security.

The methods discussed previously have laid the foundation for juror understanding of the elements involved in negligence.

Basically, negligence involves conduct. Negligence is a failure to do what the reasonable person would do "under the same or similar circumstances."[1] Jurisdictions will vary on the degrees of aggravated negligence (i.e., gross negligence) involved and amount of knowledge required on the part of a defendant to be found legally negligent. Research of the existing case law is required for each jurisdiction.

Obvious defects or absence of expected minimum security precautions required by code are often deemed as being negligence *per se* on the part of the land possessor.

Proximate Cause

The fourth element necessary to prove a tort action involving security issues is to show that inadequate security was the proximate cause of the plaintiff's assault. This connection to an act or omission on the part of a defendant is frequently disputed by both parties.

The proximate cause of an injury or cause "in fact" in a premises liability litigation is a question generally decided by a jury. One question to be answered is: Has the conduct of the defendant caused the plaintiff's loss?

Jury instructions should be prepared that explain that the alleged act or omission of a defendant *must* be closely connected to the resulting injury to the plaintiff.

Because the concept of proximate cause is often hotly disputed, many courts have developed a doctrine called the *"but for"* or *"sine qua non"* rule. This rule may be simply stated as follows: the defendant's conduct is a cause of the event if the event would not have occurred *but for* that conduct; conversely, the defendant's conduct is not a cause of the event if the event would have occurred without it.[2]

This *"but for"* rule is adequate for most cases but fails in a situation in which two or more causes concur to bring about an event, and either of them, operating alone would have caused the identical result.[3]

In other jurisdictions, proximate cause must be proven to be the "legal cause," meaning that the defendant's conduct was the *"substantial factor"* causing the plaintiff's injury. "If the defendant's act or omission was a substantial factor in bringing about the result, it will be regarded as a cause in fact"[4] In these jurisdictions, the words "legal cause" may be substituted for words "proximate cause" in the jury instructions.[5] In California, the *"substantial factor"* rule was developed to reduce confusion among jurors who often assumed the words "proximate" and "approximate" had the same meaning.[6]

Examples of proximate cause connections to a defendant might be as follows: failure to follow building codes, allowing substandard hollow doors and locking hardware to be installed in a rental apartment through which a rapist gained access; failure to provide enough trained staff to control customers in a crowded nightclub in which a fight broke out between known rival groups; failure to repair a reported defective lock that would have prevented an assailants access; and failure to use proven robbery prevention and cash handling procedures in a convenience store in which a robber shot a customer.

Examples of poor proximate cause connections to a defendant might include the following: failure to provide adequate outside lighting in a daytime assault case; failure to provide a security guard in a shopping plaza after business hours to prevent a parking lot robbery; failure to provide a key control system to prevent unauthorized key access where the door to the room was left unlocked by the guest; and failure to trim ground level bushes to prevent concealment of an assailant in a third-floor assault case.

It is generally improper for a security expert to testify as to the proximate cause issue when the facts are in dispute. An expert can only evaluate the security measures in place and give an opinion as to the adequacy of those measures.

However, hypotheticals are sometimes used as a method of providing testimony using similar circumstances to draw out opinions on the causation issue and the probability of a security precaution preventing the assault. This technique can also be used effectively by a defense attorney to show that it is sometimes impossible to predict whether the presence or absence of a particular security measure would have prevented or caused a plaintiff's injury.

Conclusion

Preparing for trial in a premises liability case involving security issues should include a method for presenting these complex issues to a jury. Rather than relying on the background and experience of individual jurors, trial attorneys should take the time to educate and train jurors on the topics of legal duty, foreseeability, adequacy, and security methodology.

Each subject can be discussed briefly but with enough detail to provide real training for the jurors. This training can be made in the form of presentations utilizing available witnesses as well as opening and closing statements.

Along with proving or disproving the elements of the tort being litigated, this presentation format will provide the jury with valuable criteria upon which to base its decision. Without such a criteria, jurors may decide a case based on erroneous beliefs or on the whim of other jurors.

Professional quality visual aids are important in the understanding of the concepts and retention of the facts presented. Charts and graphs should be screened for inadmissibility potential prior to attempted use in court.

A security expert should be utilized fully during the trial preparation phase and assist in planning the most effective ways to present the material to the court. The expert who participates in a professional presentation will usually be viewed as knowledgeable and credible by a jury.

Use this book as a constant reference and guide to aid in the evaluation of any property open to the public. It is hoped that this book will greatly enhance the way you view security liability issues in the future.

ENDNOTES

1. William L. Prosser, *Prosser and Keeton on the Law of Torts*, 5th ed., ed. W. Page Keeton (St. Paul, Minn.: West Publishing Co., 1984), 175, quoting Rest.2d Torts, Section 283. (*See also*, Prosser, Proximate Cause in California, 1950, 38 *Cal.L.Rev.* p.369)
2. Prosser, *Law of Torts*, 266.
3. *Vesely v. Sager*, 5 Cal.3d 153, 163, 95 Cal.Rptr. 623, 630, 486 P.2d 151 (1971)
4. Barclay Kitchen, Inc. v. California Bank, 208 Cal.App.2d 347,354, 25 Cal.Rptr. 383,387 (1962)
5. *Cal.Jury Inst.Civ.* 7th ed., BAJI 3.76, (St. Paul, Minn.: West Publishing Co., 1986).
6. Rest.2d Torts, section 431.

Amir, M. *Patterns in Forcible Rape*. Chicago: The University of Chicago Press, 1971.

Angel, S. *Discouraging Crime Through City Planning*. Berkeley, CA: University of California, Institute of Urban and Regional Development, Center for Planning & Development, Working Paper No. 75, 1968.

Anthony, Andrew J., and F.F. Thornburg. "Liability Lessons: Security on Trial," *Security Management*. Feb. 33, 2 (1989): 40-46.

Baldwin, J., and A. E. Bottoms. *The Urban Criminal: A Study in Sheffield*. London: Tavistock Publications, 1976.

Boggs, S. "Urban Crime Patterns." *American Sociological Review* 30 (1966): 899-908.

Bottom, Norman R., Jr., PhD. *Security, Loss Control, Negligence*. Columbia, MD: Hanrow Press, 1985.

_____. *The Parking Lot and Garage Security Handbook*. Columbia, MD: Hanrow Press, 1988.

Brantingham, P. J., D. A. Dyreson, and P. L. Brantinham. "Crime Seen Through a Cone of Resolution." *American Behavioral Scientist* 20, 2 (1976): 261-273.

Brantingham, P., and P. Brantingham. *Patterns in Crime.* New York, NY: Macmillan Publishing Company, 1984.

_____, eds. *Environmental Criminology.* Beverly Hills, CA: Sage Publications, 1981.

Broder, J. F. *Risk Analysis and the Security Survey.* Boston and London: Butterworth Publishers, 1984.

Bullock, H. A. "Urban Homicide in Theory and Fact." *Journal of Criminal Law, Criminology and Police Science* Jan. (1955): 565-575.

Burstein, Harvey. *Management of Hotel and Motel Security.* New York, NY: Marcel Dekker, Inc., 1980.

Cabrera, S. A. "Negligence Liability of Landowners and Occupiers for the Criminal Conduct of Another: On a Clear Day in California One Can Foresee Forever." *California Western Law Review* 23, 2 (1987): 165-191.

Capone, D. L. and W. W. Nichols, Jr. "Urban Structure and Criminal Mobility." *American Behavioral Scientist* 20, 2 (1976): 199-213.

Carroll, J. M. *Managing Risk, A Computer-Aided Strategy.* Stoneham, MA: Butterworth Publishers, 1984.

Carter, Ronald L. "The Criminal's Image of the City and Urban Crime Patterns," *Social Science Quarterly*, 57, (1976): 597-607.

Citizens Crime Commission of New York City, and Regional Plan Association. *Downtown Safety, Security and Economic Development.* New York, NY: Downtown Research & Development Center, 1985.

Crow, Wayman J., PhD & Bull, James L., PhD. *Robbery Deterrence: An Applied Behavioral Science Demonstra-*

tion. Western Behavioral Sciences Institute, La Jolla, CA. , 1975.

Davidson, R. N. *Crime and Environment.* New York, NY: St. Martin's Press, 1981.

Duffala, D. "Convenience Stores, Armed Robbery and Physical Environmental Features." *American Behavioral Scientist* 20, 2 (1976): 227-246.

Ellis, Raymond C., Jr. *Security and Loss Prevention Management.* East Lansing, MI: Educational Institute of the Hotel & Motel Association, 1986.

Farmer, David J., *Crime Control, The Use and Misuse of Police Resources.* New York, NY: Plenum Press, 1984.

Farrinton, David P., L.E. Ohlin, and J.Q. Wilson. *Understanding and Controlling Crime, Toward a New Research Strategy.* New York, NY: Springer-Verlag, 1986.

Federal Bureau of Investigation. *Crime in the United States, Uniform Crime Reports.* Washington, DC: U.S. Department of Justice, F. B. I., published annually.

Feeney, F. *The Prevention and Control of Robbery.* Davis, CA: University of California, Center on Administration of Justice, 1973.

Fowler, F. J., Jr., and T. Mangione. *Neighborhood Crime, Fear and Social Control.* Washington, DC: U.S. Department of Justice, Law Enforcement Assistance Administration, National Institute of Law Enforcement and Criminal Justice, 1982.

_____, M. E. McCalla, and T. W. Mangione. *Reducing Residential Crime and Fear: The Hartford Neighborhood Crime Prevention Program.* Washington, DC: U.S. Department of Justice, Law Enforcement Assistance

Administration, National Institute of Law Enforcement and Criminal Justice, 1979.

Gigliotti, R. J., and R. C. Jason. *Security Design for Maximum Protection*. Stoneham, MA: Butterworth Publishers, 1984.

Gabor, T. "The Crime Displacement Hypothesis: An Empirical Examination." *Crime & Delinquency* (July, 1981): 390-404.

Goldstein, Herman. *Policing a Free Society*. Cambridge, MA: Ballinger Publishing Company, 1977.

Greenberg, S. W., W. M. Rohe, and J. R. Williams. *Safe and Secure Neighborhoods: Physical Characteristics and Informal Territorial Control in High and Low Crime Neighborhoods*.

Grose, V. L. *Managing Risk*. Englewood Cliffs, N J: Prentice Hall, 1987.

Hagan, J., ed. *Deterrence Reconsidered, Methodological Innovations*. Beverly Hills, CA: Sage Publications, 1982.

Harlow, C. W. *Robbery Victims*. Washington, DC: U.S. Department of Justice, Bureau of Justice Statistics, Special Report, 1987.

Hughes, D. R., and G. R. Cooper. *Building Security Standards, Final Report to the California Legislature*. State of California: Department of Justice, Attorney General's Building Security Commission, 1974.

Hughes, M. K. "Premise Liability and Third-Party Criminal Conduct." *The Bulletin*, South Carolina Trial Lawyers Association (May/June, 1986): 5-9.

Illuminating Engineering Society of North America. *IES Lighting Handbook.* New York: IES Publications, published annually. (See also other IES publications).

Inciardi, J. A. "The Uniform Crime Reports: Some Considerations on Their Shortcomings and Utility." *Public Data Use* 6, 6 (Nov., 1978), 3-16.

International Conference of Building Officials. *Uniform Building Security Code.* Whittier, CA: I. C. B. O., 1979, 1985.

International Council of Shopping Centers. *Security & Safety, Issues and Ideas for Shopping Center Professionals.* New York, NY: I.C.S.C., 1989.

Jacobs, J. *The Death and Life of Great American Cities.* New York, NY: Vintage Books, 1961.

Jefferies, Jack P. *Understanding Hotel/Motel Law.* East Lansing, MI: Educational Institute of the American Hotel & Motel Association, 1983.

Jeffery, C. R. "Criminal Behavior and the Physical Environment." *American Behavioral Scientist* 20, 2 (1976): 149-174.

Jenkins, P. *Crime and Justice, Issues and Ideas.* Monterey, CA: Brooks/Cole Publishing Company, 1984.

Kennedy, Daniel B., PhD. "Case Your Space". *Security Management.* 33, 4 Apr. (1989): 47-52.

Langan, P. A., and C. A. Innes. *The Risk of Violent Crime.* Washington, DC: U.S. Department of Justice, Bureau of Justice Statistics Special Report, 1985.

Law Enforcement Assistance Administration. *Physical Security of Door Assemblies and Components.*

Washington, DC: U. S. Department of Justice, Law Enforcement Assistance Administration, 1975.

Lawrence, G. G., M. Dabertin, and S. M. Ray. "Landlord Liability for Criminal Acts of Third Parties." *For the Defense* Dec. (1986): 16-24.

Mawby, R. I. "Defensible Space: A Theoretical and Empirical Appraisal." *Urban Studies* 14 (1977): 169-179.

Mawson, A. *Transient Criminality.* New York, NY: Praeger, 1987.

McIver, John P. "Criminal Mobility: A Review of Empirical Studies," *Crime Spillover*, eds. Simon Hakim and George Rengert. Beverly Hills, CA: Sage Publications, 1981

Megargee, E. I. "Psychological Determinants and Correlates of Criminal Violence." In *Criminal Violence*, edited by M. E. Wolfgang, and N. A. Weiner, 81-162. Beverly Hills, CA: Sage Publications, 1982.

Milich, M. F. "Protecting Commercial Landlords From Liability for Criminal Acts of Third Parties." *Real Estate Law Journal* 15 (1987): 236.

Molumby, T. "Patterns of Crime in a University Housing Project," *American Behavioral Scientist* 20, 2 (1976): 247-259.

Morris, T. *The Criminal Area*: A Study in Social Ecology. London, England: Routledge & Kegan Paul, 1958.

National Institute of Law Enforcement and Criminal Justice. *Federal Security Code with Minimum Building Security Guidelines and Cost Estimates for the Security Features.* Washington, DC: Law Enforcement Assistance Administration, 1971.

Newman, O. *Architectural Design for Crime Prevention.* Washington, DC: U.S. Department of Justice, Law Enforcement Assistance Administration, National Institute of Law Enforcement and Criminal Justice, 1973.

_____. *Defensible Space.* New York, NY: Macmillan Publishing Co., Inc., 1973.

_____. *Design Guidelines for Creating Defensible Space.* Washington, DC: U. S. Department of Justice, Law Enforcement Assistance Administration, National Institute of Law Enforcement and Criminal Justice, 1976.

_____, and K. Franck. *Factors Influencing Crime and Instability in Urban Housing Developments.* Washington DC: U. S. Department of Justice, National Institute of Justice, 1980.

_____, and S. Johnston. *Model Security Codes for Residential Areas.* New York, NY: Institute for Community Design Analysis, 1974.

Pascal, A. Michael. *Hospital Security and Safety.* Rockville, MD: Aspen Systems Corporation, 1977

Pettiway, Leon. "Mobility of Robbery and Burglary Offenders: Ghetto and Nonghetto Spaces," *Urban Affairs Quarterly*, 18, (1982): 255-270.

Peyrat, P. *California Tort Guide.* Berkeley, CA: Continuing Education of the Bar, 1985.

Pope, C. E. "Patterns in Burglary: An Empirical Examination of Offense and Offender Characteristics." *Journal of Criminal Justice* 8 (1980): 39-51.

Poyner, B. *Design Against Crime.* London, England: Butterworths, 1983.

Poynter, Daniel F. *The Expert Witness Handbook, Tips and Techniques for the Litigation Consultant.* Santa Barbara, CA: Para Publishing, 1987.

Pyle, G. F. "Spatial and Temporal Aspects of Crime in Cleveland, Ohio." *American Behavioral Scientist* 20, 2 (1976): 175-197.

Reiss, A. J., Jr. *The Police and the Public.* New Haven, CT: Yale University Press, 1971.

Repetto, T. A. *Residential Crime.* Cambridge, MA: Ballinger Publishing Company, 1974.

_____. "Crime Prevention and the Displacement Phenomenon." *Crime & Delinquency* Apr. (1976): 166-177.

_____. "Crime Prevention Through Environmental Policy." *American Behavioral Scientist* 20, 2 (1976): 275-288.

Rubenstein, H., C. Murray, T. Motoyama, W. V. Rouse, and R. M. Titus. *Link Between Crime and the Built Environment: The Current State of Knowledge.* Washington, DC: U.S. Department of Justice, National Institute of Justice, 1980.

Sagalyn, A. *The Crime of Robbery in the United States.* Washington, DC: U.S. Department of Justice, Law Enforcement Assistance Administration, National Institute of Law Enforcement and Criminal Justice, 1971.

Shaw, C. R., and H. D. McKay. *Juvenile Delinquency and Urban Areas.* Chicago, IL: University of Chicago Press, 1969.

Sherman, L. W. *Protecting Customers From Crime.* Washington, DC: Security Law Institute, 1984.

_____, and J. Klein. *Major Lawsuits Over Crime and Security: Trends and Patterns, 1958-1982.* College Park, MD: University of Maryland, Institute of Criminal Justice and Criminology, 1984.

Spain, N. M. "Inadequate Security and Negligent Hiring." Paper presented at Research Security Administrators Conference, SRI International, Menlo Park, CA, April 1987.

Tarras, John, JD. *Reducing Liability costs in the Lodging Industry, A Planned Approach to Risk Management.* East Lansing, MI: Educational Institute of the American Hotel & Motel Association, 1986.

Task Force on Private Security. *Private Security.* Washington, DC: National Advisory Committee on Criminal Justice Standards & Goals, 1976.

Taub, R. P., G. Taylor, and J. D. Dunham. *Crime, Fear of Crime, and the Deterioration of Urban Neighborhoods, Executive Summary.* Washington, DC: U.S. Department of Justice, National Institute of Justice, 1982.

Tien, J. M., V. F. O'Donnell, A. Barnett, and P. M. Mirchandani. *Street Lighting Projects.* Washington, DC: U.S. Department of Justice, Law Enforcement Assistance Administration, National Institute of Law Enforcement and Criminal Justice, 1979.

Underwood, G. *The Security of Buildings.* London, England: The Architectural Press, 1984.

Walker, Samuel. *Sence and Nonsence About Crime, A Policy Guide.* Pacific Grove, CA: Brooks/Cole Publishing Company, 1989.

Waller, I., and N. Okihiro. *Burglary: The Victim and the Public*. Toronto: University of Toronto Press, 1978.

Wallis, A., and D. Ford, *Crime Prevention Through Environmental Design: The School Demonstration in Broward County, Florida, Executive Summary*. Washington, DC: U. S. Department of Justice, National Institute of Justice, 1980.

Weiss, J. L. "Landlord Liability—Obligation to Maintain Adequate Security—A Comparative Study." *Tulane Law Review* 59 (1985): 701-746.

White, R. C. "The Relation of Felonies to Environmental Factors in Indianapolis." *Social Forces* 10 (1932): 498-509.

Wilcox, S., *The Prevention and Control of Robbery*, Vol. III, *The Geography of Robbery*. Edited by Feeney, and Weir. Davis, CA: University of California, 1974.

William Brill Associates, Inc. *Planning for Security, Site Security Analysis Manual*. Washington, DC: U.S. Department of Housing and Urban Development, Office of Policy Development and Research, 1979.

Wilson, J. Q. *Crime and Public Policy*. San Francisco, CA: Institute for Contemporary Studies, 1983.

_____. *Thinking About Crime*. New York, NY: Basic Books, Inc., 1975.

Yeager, Robert. *The Failure to Provide Security Handbook, Building and Parking Lots*. Columbia, MD: Hanrow Press, 1986.

Yochelson, S., and S. E. Samenow. *The Criminal Personality*, Vol. I , *A Profile for Change*. New York, NY: Jason Aronson, 1976.

SUITABLE FOR A SHOPPING CENTER MATTER

Provide the following materials to your security expert:

1. Litigation complaint including points and authorities in support of each allegation.

2. All written arguments containing relevant facts or disputes, motions for and against summary judgement and all pleadings relevant to security issues.

3. Complete copies of all police incident reports and follow-up investigative reports, including any photographs and/or crime scene sketches. Descriptions or photographs of any relevant physical evidence still in police custody.

4. All interrogatory questions and responses relating to factual and security issues.

5. Copies of all leases involving the premises owner and any lessee, licensee, franchisee, contractor or other entities in the litigation.

6. A relevant site plan of the premises including scale dimensions, identified buildings and tenants, property boundaries and other physical attributes. Provide a lighting diagram of the area where the incident occurred, if a night incident.

7. All requests for discovery relating to factual and security issues and a list of materials provided.

8. All relevant deposition or preliminary hearing transcripts involving factual information and security issues.

9. Names and addresses of the opposing security experts and other professional witnesses. Obtain resumes or declarations of experience and expected testimony.

10. Police crime statistics for the premises and the surrounding area (the smallest available police reporting beat, area or district) for the relevant year and two preceding years.

11. All internal security incident and daily activity reports and/or internal management reports of crimes, incidents and other security activities for the relevant year and two preceding years.

12. Copies of any outside contract security service agreements, and any documentation (ie. post orders, guard activity reports, schedules, etc.) from the guard contractor.

13. If off-duty law enforcement officers were used, copies of any ordinances and departmental regulations governing off-duty employment, and any correspondence with the law enforcement agency regarding protection of the premises.

14. All correspondence and inquiries involving local law enforcement agencies regarding criminal activity and/or security at the facility, including any police crime prevention surveys or programs offered.

15. All security manuals, directives, policies and procedures, orders and instructions, memoranda, etc., relating to security of the relevant area.

16. All training materials and policies used to teach and inform security personnel and records/verification of those who received training.

17. Personnel files of all security staff assigned to the premises on the day of the incident.

18. Copies of operations and security budgets for the fiscal year and two preceding fiscal years. Business financial statement to show percent of security budget.

19. Security staffing schedules for the relevant month and six preceding months along with any security attendance records, time cards and/or other records.

20. Description and number of all vehicles used for parking lot security patrol, equipment carried and whether they were operational at the time of the incident.

21. Description of any security communications systems (two- way radio, intercom, pager, etc.) in use on the day of the incident.

22. Description of any electronic security surveillance systems (closed circuit television, audio monitoring, access controls, intrusions alarms, etc.) in use on the day of the incident.

23. Any internal security inspections, surveys, and/or audits or other reports made by the corporate office or outside consultants, prior to this incident.

24. Copies of minutes of any merchants association, tenants association and/or security/safety committee meetings at which security was discussed, and any association correspondence regarding security.

25. Copies of complaints received from tenants, residents, employees, guests and/or business invitees regarding security issues in the relevant area.

26. Newspaper articles, photographs, audio/video tapes or other media items relevant to the site and security issues.

27. Any information regarding subsequent security improvements made since the incident. Subsequent improvements may be admissible under certain conditions.

INTERROGATORIES

SUITABLE FOR A SHOPPING CENTER MATTER

These questions are only guidelines designed to stimulate ideas to aid in the development of more effective interrogatories. Please consult other legal resources for precise language, writing style, and form.

Assume a parking lot assault case:

1. Names and addresses of all property owners, lessees, franchisees, vendors, contractors, and management companies involved with the relevant area for (the specific time period) and for six months prior to the incident?

2. Names and addresses, and titles of all personnel or entities ultimately responsible for management and supervision of the parking lot area for (the specific time period) and for six months prior to the incident?

3. Names, addresses, and titles of all persons directly responsible for managing the parking lot security function for (the specific time period) and for six months preceding the incident?

4. Names, addresses, and titles of all employees who performed a security function in the parking lot for (the specific time period) and for six months prior to the incident?

5. Describe the minimum criteria and qualifications used to hire the above named persons who performed the security function (i.e., guard card, license, permit), the extent of any background verification, and the location of their employment files?

6. Describe the security training provided to each person, the name of who provided the security training, (whether it was in written form or verbal), and the names and location of all written training materials utilized?

7. Names and addresses of all contractors and their employees who provided any security services to the shopping center for (the specific time period) and for six months prior to the incident?

8. Identify any written agreements or contracts between any parties regarding security in the shopping center parking lot area and the location of said documents.

9. Describe the type and quantity of all vehicles used for parking lot security patrol, equipment carried, and whether they were operational at the time of the incident?

10. Describe the type and number of security communications devices in use (i.e., two-way radio, intercom, pager, etc.) in the parking area on the date of the incident and whether they were operational?

11. Describe the type and number of any electronic security surveillance systems in the parking area (i.e., closed circuit video, audio monitoring, access controls, intrusion detectors, etc) in use on the date of the incident?

12. Names of the security personnel who were on duty and on the shopping center property on the date and time period of the incident?

13. Describe how the above staff were deployed around the shopping center: what duties did they perform, what equipment did they carry, and what vehicles, if any, did they utilize?

14. Identify the security supervisors, if any, and what duties they performed on the date and time of the incident?

15. Identify the names of the reports, if any, that security personnel use to document their daily activities, specific incidents, items in need of repair, and other notifications and the name and address of the custodian of said records and the physical location of the records?

16. Identify any summary reports, crime statistics, and/or analysis of the shopping center security department activity to supervisors, corporate management, or crime committees submitted prior to the date of this incident.

17. Identify any criminal incidents (either property or assaultive) occurring in the parking lot area and reported to any shopping center, security, or contract security personnel on or before the date of this incident?

18. State the date, time, location, report number, and nature of each reported incident for a two year period prior to the date of this incident.

19. Has any surveys been conducted by any security consultant, police officer, employee, or investigator to determine the level of crime foreseeability or vulnerability to criminal activity in the parking area prior to the date of the incident?

20. If so, state surveyors name and address, time and date of each survey, and present location of physical survey report?

21. Does the shopping center or merchant association have a security or safety committee?

22. Name and address of the person in charge of that committee on the date of this incident?

23. Names and addresses of members of this committee and of any private person who has filed written complaints regarding parking lot crime and other security issues to any shopping center personnel?

24. Names and addresses of anyone who has taken photographs of the parking lot area depicting any criminal activity or security hazard prior to the date of the incident.

SUITABLE FOR A SECURITY EXPERT WITNESS

These questions are only guidelines designed to stimulate ideas to aid in the development of more effective voir dire inquires of security expert's. Please consult other legal resources for advise on proper voir dire of an expert.

BACKGROUND

Full legal name?

Current business address and telephone?

Date of birth and social security number?

When was the witness first contacted by counsel regarding this case?

When did the witness decide to testify as an expert witness in this case?

What is the scope of the assignment for the witness as an expert in this case?

What work has the witness performed to date including materials reviewed?

What tests and experiments have been performed by the witness for this case?

In what areas does witness claim to be an expert?

Number of times testified as a security expert in either a trial or deposition?

Has the witness ever testified in a case involving a retail store parking lot assault?

Names of states, counties, and courts where testified?

Names of cases, attorneys, cities, dates and nature of testimony?

Number and nature of plaintiff cases worked as an expert?

Number and nature of defense cases worked as an expert?

How much is the witness being paid to testify as an expert?

How many hours has the witness worked to date on the case?

Does the witness intend to do any more work on the case?

Has the witness formed final opinions in this case?

EMPLOYMENT HISTORY (review resume)

Name and address of present employer?

Name of supervisor?

Date hired?

Describe the nature of the business?

Is the business a corporation, partnership, etc?

Title or position held?

Describe security responsibilities?

Name and address of immediately preceding employer?

Dates hired/left?

Names of supervisor?

Reason for leaving?

Describe the business?

Title or position held?

Describe security responsibilities?

(Continue through employment history using the same questions as above until all prior experience is reviewed).

Any military service, branch, dates, where stationed, major job assignment?

Where discharged, rank on discharge, type of discharge?

Any disciplinary action (ie. Article 15, Captain's Mast)?

CASE SPECIFIC SECURITY EXPERIENCE

Has the witness ever designed security systems?

Has the witness ever written security manuals?

Has the witness ever managed security programs?

Has the witness ever supervised a security staff or guard force?

Has the witness ever conducted security surveys on a retail premises before?

Has the witness ever performed crime demographic research before?

Any of the above experience in the retail environment?

Any of the above experience involve parking lot security?

FORMAL EDUCATION

Names, locations, and dates of colleges attended?

Describe major course of study at each college?

Identify college and type of degree obtained and date?

Any of the subject matter security related?

Ever taught a security course at a college?

LICENSES AND CERTIFICATIONS

Does the witness have any professional licenses?

Does the witness hold any professional security certifications?

PROFESSIONAL ASSOCIATIONS

Does the witness belong to any professional security associations?

Has the witness ever held office in a professional security association?

HONORS AND AWARDS

Has the witness ever been recognized by any authoritative body or professional organization for work performed in the security industry?

Where, when, what honor or award, who presented?

PUBLICATIONS

Has the witness ever published an article or book on the subject of security?

What publications, when, what was the topic?

SECURITY TRAINING

Has the witness received any specialized training in the security field for the private sector (Not law enforcement or government)?

What training, how many hours, where, when, and subject?

Has the witness attended any security trade shows?

How often, when, where, name of trade show?

SPEECHES & PRESENTATIONS

Has the witness ever given a speech on a security topic?

Where, when, to what audience, how many times?

Has the witness ever been interviewed for radio, television, or newspaper as a security expert?

GENERAL

What percentage of the total business hours does the witness spend advising or testifying for attorneys in litigation cases?

On how many cases has the witness been retained either to consult or testify as a security expert?

How many litigation cases does the witness currently have open?

What percentage of the total business hours is the witness actively involved in the practice of security?

APPENDIX

CASE REFERENCES

These case references are brief summaries of selected premises liability judgments from around the United States.

7735 Hollywood Boulevard Venture v. Superior Court, 116 Cal. App.3d 910, 172 Cal. Rptr. 528 (1981).

Tenant brought action to recover for injuries sustained in rape by an intruder who forced entrance into her apartment. The plaintiff alleged that the property owner had knowledge that violent crime, including burglary and rape, had occurred in the "general area" and provided inadequate lighting by failure to replace burned out bulbs outside her apartment. The Court of Appeal held that the tenant's complaint failed to plead sufficient facts to create any duty on the part of the owner of the apartment building to protect the tenant from criminal acts of third parties or to establish any causal connection between alleged defect and injuries sustained by the tenant.

Ballew v. Southland Corp., 462 So.2d 890 (La. 1986).

Convenience store customer sued store for failure to provide adequate security to protect its customers; for violating its own safety practices designed to protect customers; and for violation of a Shreveport city ordinance. Ballew stopped at a 7-Eleven at night and encountered a large man loitering around the front of the store. After waiting for this man to leave Ballew entered the store. The man suddenly reappeared and followed Ballew into the store while asking her for money or merchandise. The store clerk asked the man to leave, at which time the man forcibly dragged Ballew from the store and raped her. The clerk was aware of this man bothering other customers for at least 30 minutes prior to Ballew's assault. The trial court awarded damages to Ballew. The Southland Corporation appealed based on the theory that it owed no duty to the plaintiff for unforeseeable acts committed by a third party. The appellate court upheld the judgment of the lower court believing that the risk of harm was known and that prevention of that harm was reasonably within their power (i.e. use of the telephone), and therefore such a duty of protection would exist.

Banks v. Hyatt Corp., 722 F.2d 214 (5th Cir. 1984).

The estate of a murdered hotel guest brought action against a hotel. The Supreme Court held that: (1) innkeepers should take measures of protection within their power and capacity and those that can reasonably be expected to mitigate the risk of criminal attacks by intruders; (2) that an innkeeper had a duty to protect those parts of its premises that are not periodically patrolled and inspected by the police; and (3) that liability for criminal activity extended to areas adjacent to the premises where landlord had sufficient control and was capable of taking reasonable action.

Basso v. Miller, 40 N.Y.2d 233, 386 N.Y.S.2d 564, 352 N.E.2d 863 (1976).

Passenger in a motorcycle accident sued the motorcycle driver and landowner for injuries sustained while drive on a private road containing potholes that upset the motorcycle. The Court of Appeals held: (1) for a new trial in which a single standard of care should applied without distinction among licensees, trespassers, and invitees; (2) the duty of a landowner should not vary with the person using the property, but he should act reasonably to maintain safe conditions in view of all the circumstances, the likelihood of injury, the seriousness thereof and the burden of avoiding the risk, and the likelihood the plaintiff's presence should be a primary *independent* factor in determining foreseeability.

Becker v. I.R.M. Corp., 38 Cal.3d 454, 698 P.2d 116, 213 Cal.Rptr. 213 (1985).

Tenant brought a personal injury lawsuit against a landlord after falling against an untempered glass shower door. Tenant asserted strict liability and negligence. The Supreme Court held that: (1) landlord engaged in business of leasing dwellings could be held strictly liable in tort for injuries resulting from latent defect in premises when defect existed at time premise were let to tenant; and (2) landlord could properly be found to be under a duty, in exercise of due care, to inspect for dangerous conditions in connection with purchase of rental premises which, at time of purchase, contained untempered glass shower doors in some of apartments, and lack of awareness of that dangerous condition would not necessarily preclude liability.

Bigbee v. Pacific Telephone & Telegraph Co. 665 P.2d 947, 34 Cal.3d 49, 192 Cal.Rptr. 857 (Sup. 1983).

A telephone booth user who was injured when an automobile jumped the curb and struck him, sued the telephone company and others. The phone booth was located in the corner parking lot of a liquor store and within 15 feet of a major thoroughfare. The plaintiff observed a vehicle veer off the road directly towards him and the phone booth. The door to the booth allegedly jammed, trapping the plaintiff inside. Summary judgment in favor of the defendant was granted. On appeal the appellate court held that substantial fact issues existed as the foreseeability of risk for a user of the telephone booth, from which it was difficult to exit, and was placed in a parking lot too near a thoroughfare and driveway. The decision was reversed and remanded.

Brown v. Maxey, 369 N.W.2d 677, 124 Wis.2d 426 (1985).

A suit was brought by a tenant who was badly burned in a fire of suspicious origins. The Wisconsin Supreme Court held that evidence of uncorrected and serious security problems coupled with a history of criminal acts on the premises permitted the jury to determine that the building owner exhibited conduct in reckless and conscious disregard of the plaintiff's rights and safety.

Cappaert v. Junker, 413 So.2d 378 (Miss. 1982).

A tenant brought action against a landlord for injuries sustained after slipping and falling down the common area staircase. The landlord introduced the tenant's lease which contained exculpatory provisions to protect the landlord from liability. Judgment was entered in favor of the landlord and the tenant appealed. The Supreme Court held that an exculpatory clause, insofar as it tried to protect the landlord from damages caused by his own negligence in maintaining the common area, was void as against public policy.

Carmichael v. Colonial Square Apartments, 38 Ohio App.3d 131 (1987).

Tenant sued landlord after being assaulted and robbed inside his second floor apartment. Tenant responded to the doorbell one evening and opened the door without looking through the peephole or securing the safety chain. An intruder with a shotgun forced his way into the apartment. Tenant alleged that inadequate security in the common area and failure to complete an installation of an exterior door access system. The court held that the landlord did take reasonable steps by equipping apartments with two locks, a peephole and safety chain and was in the process of adding a exterior door access system.

Carrigan v. New World Enters., Ltd., 112 Ill.App.3d 970, 446 N.E.2d 265 (1985).

Tenant sued landlord and its agents for injuries resulting from rape by an intruder. The landlord advertised that each apartment had a burglar alarm system. The plaintiff complained that her alarm was defective although stated that she rarely used it anyway. The Appellate Court held that although the landlord installed a burglar alarm and had contracted to keep it operable, landlord's breach did not render it liable for injuries plaintiff received while alarm was not activated by the tenant.

Cohen v. Southland Corp., 157 Cal.App.3d 130, 203 Cal.Rptr. 572 (1984).

A convenience store customer was abducted from the parking lot as he drove up, by a gunman who intended to rob the store, take Cohen hostage, and flee using his car. Once inside the store the robber proceeded to demand money from the lone 7-Eleven clerk when Cohen attempted to grab the robber from behind. Cohen was shot while the clerk retreated to the back room and barricaded himself inside. The clerk did not call the police. Cohen subsequently sued the clerk, the franchisee, and Southland Corporation for failure to protect patrons from criminal attack and for the clerk's failure to take action after the shooting. The trial court granted summary judgment based on testimony only one prior similar act did not make this crime foreseeable. On appeal the Appellate court reversed and remanded the case for trial based on a review of the evidence that a triable issue existed. The court commented that 7-Eleven robberies at other locations raise a question of fact as to whether future armed robberies might be reasonably foreseeable.

C.S. v. Sophir, 20 Neb. 51, 368 N.W.2d 444 (1985).

Action was brought against landlord by tenant who was sexually assaulted in parking lot of apartment complex. The plaintiff alleged that the landlord had actual knowledge of another sexual assault that occurred just two months prior in the same parking lot and failed to warn her of the danger and also claimed inadequate lighting and excessive growth of shrubbery in the area. The trial court dismissed the case for failure to state a cause of action. The plaintiff appealed. The Supreme Court held that (1) the landlord did not have a duty to warn tenants of the danger of sexual assault in parking area; and (2) failure of landlord to clear weeds from areas adjacent to parking lot and his failure to provide adequate lighting did not constitute active negligence but mere conditions of negligence.

Deeds v. American Sec., 39 Ohio App.3d 31 (1987).

A guest of an apartment tenant was accosted in the parking lot and raped. While the rape was in progress a security guard employed by the apartment complex drove by and observed what he perceived to be a consensual sexual act, and advised the couple that behavior of that nature would not be tolerated. The guard left, promising to return. The plaintiff filed suit against the guard and guard company for negligent execution of his duties. The court held that the security guard had no duty to protect persons on the premises and had only to fulfill the terms of the contract and exercise ordinary care in the performance of his duties. The security contract specified the purpose of the patrol was only to reduce vandalism and crime against property not against persons.

Dick v. Great S. Bay Co., 106 Misc.2d 686, 435 N.Y.S.2d 240 (1981)

Tenant sued the landlord for injuries sustained from a criminal attack on the premises. Three assailants entered via the front common area door of an apartment building and robbed and assaulted the plaintiff who was waiting for the elevator in the lobby. The door lock had been in disrepair for more than one year despite numerous complaints from the tenants. The plaintiff received a favorable jury verdict and the landlord filed a motion to set aside the verdict and dismiss the complaint. The court held that even though the plaintiff failed to produce evidence of prior criminal activities in the area, the jury could determine by its own "common experience" the relationship between the defective door lock and violent criminal activity occurring throughout the city. The court stated that the cost to repair a lock was a reasonable expected step compared to the potential danger to the tenants.

Feld v. Merriam, 485 A.2d 742, 506 Pa. 383 (1984).

Apartment tenants where kidnapped from the building's garage and assaulted. The court stated that a program of security is not the usual and normal precaution that a reasonable home owner would employ to protect his property. Therefore, the landlord had no general duty to protect the tenants from criminal intrusion, unless he had taken on the duty voluntarily or by specific agreement.

Foster v. Winston-Salem Joint Venture, 274 S.E.2d 265, 281 S.E.2d 36, 50 N.C.App. 516 (1981).

A patron was assaulted and robbed in the parking lot of a shopping mall. While returning to her car, two unidentified males beat and robbed the plaintiff. Suit was brought claiming that the shopping mall was negligent in failing to provide adequate security in the parking lot. The plaintiff produced evidence of 29 previous criminal incidents in the preceding year, of which only 4-5 involved assaultive behavior. The trial court granted summary judgment to the defendants. On appeal the court held that substantial fact issues existed as to the foreseeability of criminal acts in the mall parking lot, which would create a duty in mall owners to provide adequate protection for their customers. Judgment affirmed in part, reversed in part, and remanded.

Frances T. v. Village Green Owners Ass'n, 723 P.2d 573, 42 Cal.3d 490, 229 Cal.Rptr. 456, (1986).

Condominium owner sued her owner's association for negligence regarding injuries she sustained when she was attacked in her unit. The plaintiff complained of inadequate lighting outside her unit after being burglarized. Requests for more exterior lighting to the owner's association were ignored. The plaintiff installed her own lights but was forced by the association to remove them because it violated the rules. She was robbed and raped inside her apartment after she was forced by the association to have the lights turned off. The trial court dismissed the case. The California Supreme Court reversed and held that the condominium association performed the functions of a landlord and owed the unit owner the same duty as a landlord owes to a tenant for the safety of common areas under the association's control.

Gomez v. Ticor, 145 Cal.App.3d 622, 193 Cal.Rptr. 600 (1983).

Actions were brought to recover for alleged wrongful death of business patron who was fatally shot when he was robbed while returning to his car, parked in an office building's commercial parking structure. Summary judgement was awarded to the defendant. The court of appeal reversed and held that: (1) material fact issue existed as to foreseeability of the attack, and whether operator had taken minimal precautions to protect deceased from the attack, precluding summary judgment; and (2) the foreseeability alleged would support a minimal duty to provide a first line of defense and that factual triable issues remain.

Green Cos. v. Di Vincenzo, 432 So.2d 86 (Fla. 1983).

Office worker was attacked by an intruder hiding inside his leased unlocked offices after returning from the restroom. Evidence at trial proved that the office building owner had foreseen the probability of harm to its tenants, but in fact had abandoned the security measures in place even though the external crime rate was still high. Computer printouts of police records of reported crimes in the surrounding area were admissible on the issue of crime foreseeability.

Gregorian v. National Convenience Stores, 174 Cal.App.3d 944, 220 Cal.Rptr. 302 (1985).

A convenience store customer had engaged in a dispute in front of a store with two young men. The young men fled and Gregorian entered the store. The two boys returned with eight friends who attacked Gregorian inside the store and stabbed him. The trial court dismissed the case based on the belief that there was no issue of fact because the defendants owed no duty to protect a plaintiff against the unforeseeable criminal attack (gang). The appellate court affirmed the judgement granted to the defendant.

Holley v. Mount Zion Terrace Apartments, Inc., 382 So.2d 98 (Fla. 1980).

The estate of a raped and murdered tenant brought suit against a landlord for wrongful death and for failure to provide reasonable security measures in the building's common areas. The tenant was attacked in her second floor apartment by an intruder who gained entry through a window which fronted onto a common outside walkway. The plaintiff alleged failure to provide security for the common areas. Evidence produced at trial indicated a high incidence of serious crime on the premises. The apartment complex had hired uniformed armed guards in the past years and even charged each tenant an additional five dollars per month to subsidize their salaries. The years immediately proceeding the plaintiff's death the security budget was cut each year until eliminated. No security for the common areas existed at the time of the tenants murder. The trial court granted summary judgment to the defendant. The tenant's personal representative appealed. The District Court of Appeal held that: (1) the evidence concerning the past record and therefore the future foreseeability of violent crime at the landlord's premises, the prior practice of the landlord in providing armed guards, and the fact that part of the tenant's rent may have been expressly for security raised substantial fact issues precluding summary judgment; (2) the deliberate act of the rapist murderer did not constitute an independent intervening cause which served to insulate the landlord from liability; and (3) the issue of whether the landlord's alleged breach of duty as to the areas outside the apartment was a legal cause of what happened inside could not be determined on summary judgment in light of the evidence that the intruder could have entered the apartment only through a common walkway.

Isaacs v. Huntington Memorial Hosp., 38 Cal.3d 112, 695 P.2d 653, 211 Cal.Rptr. 356 (1985).

In this landmark case, a doctor brought action against hospital and its insurance carrier for injuries sustained by doctor as a result of being shot in the hospital parking lot. The trial court granted a nonsuit and summary judgment in favor of the defendant after excluding evidence of prior similar crime on the hospital. Supreme Court held that: (1) plaintiff may establish foreseeability other than by evidence of prior similar incidents on the premises; (2) trial court erred in concluding that only prior similar crimes and not crimes on any adjacent parking lots would be admissible as a matter of law and because of that ruling the doctor's assault was not foreseeable; and (3) insurance carrier could not be held liable without having ownership, possession, or control of hospital's premises.

Kenny v. Southeastern Pennsylvania Transp. Auth., 581 F.2d 351 (1978).

A lawsuit was brought against the city and transit authority by woman who was raped inside a station of city transit authority. The plaintiff, who was alone on a platform was dragged 150 feet to dark area an assaulted. The only employee on duty was inside an enclosed ticket booth with a radio playing. Shortly after the crime new lighting was added by the defendant. The Court of Appeals held that showing of insufficient lighting on subway platform and insufficient attention to conditions by the only employee on the premises supported jury's finding of negligence on part of transit authority. Testimony at trial of subsequent repair of the lights by the defendant was found to be admissible.

Kline v. 1500 Massachusetts Ave. Apartment Corp., 439 F.2d 477 (D.C. Cir. 1970).

Tenant brought action to recover for injuries sustained when she was criminally assaulted in common hallway of apartment house. When the tenant signed the lease to move in the apartment house had either a doorman, or a front desk clerk on duty and all times. Previous garage personnel also decreased leaving the entryways unprotected. The landlord had notice the a crime wave was in progress in the area. The trial court entered a judgment for the defendant. The court of Appeals reversed and held that: (1) landlord had both actual and constructive notice of crimes occurring on the premises and was under a duty of protection; and (2) the landlord established the standard of care at the time the tenant became a resident of the premises and when that same standard was not maintained, the landlord was liable for the resulting injuries to plaintiff.

Kwaitkowski v. Superior Trading Co., 123 Cal.App.3d 324, 176 Cal.Rptr. 494 (1981).

Tenant brought suit for damages sustained when she was raped, assaulted, and robbed in the dimly lit lobby of the building. The plaintiff alleged that the front door lock was defective, lights were missing, and non-guests would pander in the hallways. The building owner was alerted to defects in the building prior to her assault. The trial court dismissed the case. The Court of Appeal reversed and held that the landlords had a special duty to the tenant based on the special relationship between them, the foreseeability of the criminal attack, and the warranty of habitability implicit in the lease contract.

Lannon v. Taco Bell, Inc., 708 P.2d 1370 (Colo. 1985).

Lannon entered a Denver Taco Bell and saw a gunman behind the counter robbing the restaurant. Lannon attempted to back out of the restaurant when he bumped into a second gunman. He ran into the parking lot and was shot in the hand by the gunman. Lannon sued, and obtained a jury verdict. Taco Bell appealed. The appellate court reversed and remanded the case to be retried. The court held that every person has a duty to refrain from acts or omissions to act which may contribute to the totality of acts which cause injury to him. The facts involving Lannon's own negligence was not submitted to the jury and the court failed to give jury instructions regarding comparative negligence.

Loeser v. Nathan Hale Gardens, Inc., 73 A.D.2d 187, 425 N.Y.S.2d 104 (1980).

A lawsuit was brought against the owner and managing agent when a tenant was assaulted in the parking lot when lights required by law were not working. The parking lot lighting was controlled by a manual timer that was maladjusted causing the lights to come during the day and off at night. A local Multiple Dwelling Law required that lights be used in these parking areas. The owner was notified prior to the assault of the defective lighting condition. In addition a lock-chain device was installed at the entranceway to the parking lot which subsequently was broken and not repaired. The Supreme Court entered judgment in favor of the plaintiff. The defendants appealed. The Supreme Court

Appellate Division held that: (1) defendants were not liable on the basis that a lock-chain device installed at entrance way to parking lot had ceased to function and had not been repaired, where apparent purpose of device was not to secure tenants against kind of violent crime that occurred; and (2) whether a criminal event of the kind that occurred was foreseeable, whether defendants' failure to restore the lights was unreasonable in proportion to the danger, and whether absence of lights was a proximate cause of the injuries were jury questions.

Lopez v. McDonald's, 193 Cal.App.3d 495, 238 Cal.Rptr. 436 (1987).

Survivors and surviving family members of 32 victims of mass murder and assault at fast food restaurant brought action against restaurant. An assailant entered the fast food restaurant dressed in camouflage attire and armed with two semi-automatic rifles and a shotgun. Showing no motivation to rob the business he reloaded his weapons several times and continued to shoot innocent victims. The plaintiff's alleged that the restaurant was in a high crime area and that mass murder was foreseeable and that the presence of an unarmed security guard could have deterred the offender from committing the crime. The trial court granted a motion for summary judgment. The Court of Appeal affirmed and held that: (1) mass murder attack at a fast food restaurant was not foreseeable; (2) that the defendant restaurant had no duty to take steps to prevent an event that was inherently unforeseeable; and (3) any breach of duty on part of restaurant owner in failing to have unarmed uniformed guards on premises was not a proximate cause of the injuries sustained by plaintiffs.

Metropolitan Atlanta Rapid Transit Auth. v. Allen, 374 S.E.2d 761, 188 Ga.App. 902 (1988).

A patron of the rail system was raped in the parking lot when she returned to her car after riding the train home from work at night. The jury awarded $250,000 to Allen. On appeal the transit system claimed that the court should not have allowed the jury to hear evidence that 10 armed robberies had occurred in the same parking lot prior to Allen's assault. The transit system argued that the prior crimes were not substantially similar to the plaintiff's case since none of them involved a rape and all of them occurred during daylight hours. The appellate court upheld the trial court's decision.

Mitchell v. Pearson Enters., 697 P.2d 240 (Utah 1985).

A hotel guest was murdered inside his room and dependants brought action against the hotel for wrongful death. His assailant had either entered the room with a passkey or followed the victim into the room from the common area hallway and shot him twice in the back of the head. The plaintiff's dependants alleged inadequate security in the guest rooms and in the common area hallways and of a breach of warranties of habitability. The trial court granted summary judgment in favor of the defendants finding that there was no genuine issue of any material fact for a jury to hear. The appellate court affirmed the judgment even though the hotel brochure assured maximum security and stated that the breach of warranty must have been the direct and proximate cause of the death.

Moody v. Cawdrey & Assoc., 721 P.2d 708 (Haw. 1986).

Condominium owners and guests brought action against the owners association and managing agent to recover for damages sustained when guests were assaulted by third parties. Guest's of the condominium owner had locked the door to their unit and retired when unknown assailants gained entry through the front door and assaulted and robbed the occupants. A security guard who was supposed to patrol the building was found to have failed in his duties. The trial court entered judgment in favor of the defendant's. On appeal the Intermediate Court of Appeals held that: (1) owners association and managing agent had duty to protect condominium owners and guests from foreseeable criminal acts committed by third parties; (2) owners and guests may establish foreseeability by evidence other than prior similar criminal incidents; and (3) genuine issues of material fact existed as to whether assault was foreseeable and whether association and agent provided security in accordance with standards required of reasonable and prudent person under the same or similar circumstances, precluding summary judgment.

Morgan v. Bucks Assoc., 428 F.Supp. 546 (E.D. Pa. 1977).

The New Jersey Supreme Court held that prior nonviolent thefts should have put a shopping center on notice that parking lot assaults were foreseeable. This notice gave rise to a jury question on the duty to protect customers from attacks by third parties.

Morgan v. Dalton Management Co., 117 Ill.App.3d 815, 454 N.E.2d 57 (1983).

Tenant brought action against the landlord and her assailant to recover for injuries sustained when assailant injured the tenant in common areas of apartment building. The plaintiff suffered from acid being thrown in her face while in an elevator by the roommate of another tenant. The trial court granted the landlord's motion to dismiss. On appeal the Appellate Court affirmed and held that: (1) landlord owned no duty to prevent another tenant from injuring her as a result of the fact that the assailant tenant and anothers were alleged to have previously threatened harm to her because the connection to the premises was too tenuous; (2) a clause in lease prohibiting tenants from performing injurious or disturbing acts did not indicate a voluntary undertaking on the part of the landlord to safeguard tenants from criminal acts of one another; and (3) the landlord-tenant relationship is not the sort of special relationship which renders a landlord responsible and liable for criminal acts of a third party.

Mullins v. Pine Manor College, 449 N.E.2d 331, 389 Mass. 47 (1983).

A student brought action against an all-female college after she was raped on campus. An intruder was able to enter the fenced campus and enter a dormitory building and room undetected. The intruder kidnapped the plaintiff and walked with her off-campus through a poorly secured gate. The gate guards were unaware of any activity and evidence indicated that their patrol procedures were unsupervised. Further evidence indicated that the room locks could be slipped with a credit card. The trial court awarded judgment to the plaintiff. The defendant's appealed. The Supreme Judicial Court held that: (1) the college had a duty to provide security for its students; (2) the evidence was sufficient to sustain the conclusion that the college was negligent in performing that duty and that the negligence was the proximate cause of the student's injuries; and (3) the vice-president was not entitled to avoid liability on the grounds that he was an officer of a charitable corporation.

Mustad v. Swedish Brethren, 83 Minn. 40, 85 N.W. 913 (1901).

On June 11, 1899 the defendant gave a picnic and invited the general public, to which he sold tickets for admission. The plaintiff who was injured in a fight, claimed that the defendant sold intoxicating liquors to "ruffians and drunken people" and should have known that such liquors would be likely to cause persons to become drunk, violent and dangerous. The plaintiff further alleged that the defendant knew that his assailant was liable to drink to excess and would become an "ugly and dangerous" person and commit assaults upon others without provocation and therefore is bound to exercise reasonable care to protect his other patrons. The appellate court reversed the lower court's decision in favor of the plaintiff.

Nixon v. Mr. Property Management Co., 690 S.W.2d 546 (Tex. 1985).

A minor's mother brought action against owners and managers of an apartment building in which the minor had been raped by an unknown person who had abducted minor from elsewhere. An assailant abducted a young girl from the sidewalk and dragged her to a vacant apartment unit across the street. The vacant apartment was full of debris, had broken windows, and the front door was off its hinges. Summary judgment was granted to the defendants. On appeal the Supreme Court reversed and held that: (1) they adopted the standard of conduct imposed by ordinance governing minimum standards to which property owners should be held as defining conduct of reasonable prudent person; (2) genuine issue of material facts as to management company's breach of duty imposed by ordinance upon property owners existed, precluding summary judgment;

and (3) material question of fact as to foreseeability of crime existed, precluding summary judgment.

Noble v. Los Angeles Dodgers, Inc., 168 Cal.App.3d 912, 214 Cal.Rptr. 395 (1985).

Noble brought action against a baseball club after being injured in a fight in the stadium parking lot following the game. Two drunks in the parking lot had vomited and urinated on the plaintiff's car causing words to be exchanged between the parties. A fight started and Noble was injured. The plaintiff alleged an inadequate number and improper deployment of security guards in the parking lot. The jury awarded him damages. The Court of Appeal reversed and held that evidence was insufficient to support the judgment and failed to prove any causal connection between any negligence and the resulting injury.

O'Hara v. Western Seven Trees Corp. Intercoast Management, 75 Cal.App.3d 798, 42 Cal.Rptr. 487 (1978).

A female tenant sought compensation from her landlord and others for damages for being raped inside her apartment. The plaintiff alleged that the landlord failed to provide adequate security, failed to warn tenants of previous assaults, and of misrepresenting security measures in effect. A rapist had previously attacked several other victims in the same apartment complex. The apartment management was notified and had composite drawings of the rapist from the police. The plaintiff was assured by the apartment rental agent that the property was safe and patrolled by security guards at all times. The trial court dismissed the case in favor of the defendants. On appeal the Court of Appeal held that: (1) the complaint stated a cause of action against landlords for failure to take reasonable steps, either by warning the tenant or by providing adequate security, to protect the tenant; (2) the complaint stated allegations which, if proved, would support an action for fraud or deceit, and (3) the facts alleged in the second cause of action could support an award of punitive damages.

Orlando Executive Park, Inc. v. P. D. R., 402 So.2d 442 (Fla. 1981).

Motel guest brought action against motel and motel chain owner after she was assaulted in the motel hallway. A man who was seen loitering behind the registration office, followed the plaintiff inside the hallway of an enclosed building. He knocked her down, choked her, dragged her under a stairwell and sexually assaulted her. The plaintiff alleged inadequate security by introducing 30 prior crimes on the premises. A security guard hired previously to patrol the property had been terminated. No other security measures were in place. The motel was part of a large complex that included five office buildings, a restaurant, and an adult movie theater. The trial court awarded damages in favor of the plaintiff but directed a verdict against punitive damages. The plaintiff appealed. The District Court of Appeal held that: (1) evidence on issue whether reasonable safety measures were taken in light of numerous criminal activities on motel premises in six-month period immediately prior to attack on guest was sufficient to support finding that motel's negligence was proximate cause of guest's injuries; and (2) failure of motel to provide security measures was not such egregious conduct as to support punitive damage award. The judgment was affirmed.

Ortell v. Spencer Cos., Inc., 477 So.2d 299 (Ala. 1985).

Ortell entered a convenience store and interrupted a robbery in progress. She was taken into the store restroom and raped.Ortill sued the store and the parent company for failure to protect customers from foreseeable crimes. The trial court granted summary judgment. The Supreme Court of Alabama affirmed the lower court's decision even though the plaintiff proved that the store had five previous robberies. The court stated that there was no other evidence to show that Spencer Companies had actual or constructive notice that Ortell's assault was a probability.

Paterson v. Deeb, 472 So.2d 1210 (Fla. 1985).

Tenant brought action against landlords for compensatory and punitive damages after sexual attack in leased premises. The plaintiff leased a unit on the upper floor of a three-unit building. The only bathroom was across the hall from her apartment and in the common area. Plaintiff alleged that she complained to the landlord about the broken lock on the front and back doors and no lock on the bathroom door. A assailant hiding inside the unlocked common area bathroom assaulted and raped the plaintiff at knife point. The trial court dismissed the case for failure to state a cause of action. The plaintiff appealed. The District Court of Appeal held: (1) landlords had a mandatory duty to provide adequate locks and keys both for outside of the apartment building and for the tenant's bathroom across the hall from her apartment; (2) landlords' actual or constructive knowledge of prior similar criminal acts committed on the premises was not required to hold landlords liable; (3) allegations that the tenants had complained to landlords in the past and that neighborhood had high level of criminal activity, along with landlords' alleged violations of statutory duty to provide adequate security, stated cause of action in negligence; and (4) trial court erred in dismissing claim for punitive damages in light of landlords' alleged willful violation of their statutory duty.

Peters v. Holiday Inns, Inc., 89 Wis.2d 115, 278 N.W.2d 208 (1979).

A motel guest who was assaulted in his motel room brought action against motel. A former motel employee stole a bellboy shirt from the kitchen and knocked on the plaintiff's door claiming he had a message to deliver. Upon opening the door he was assaulted and robbed. Although the room was secure, access to the motel building was not, thereby allowing entry of the assailants. Other than the patrol of the police, no other security measures existed. The trial court granted summary judgment for the motel. On appeal the Supreme Court held that: (1) a hotel has the duty to exercise ordinary care to provide adequate protection for its guests and their property from assaultive and other types of criminal activity; (2) in meeting its standard of ordinary care, a hotel must provide security commensurate with the facts and circumstances that are or should be apparent to the ordinarily prudent person; (3) material issues of fact existed, precluding entry of summary judgment; and (4) the fortuitous presence of the police did not, as a matter of law, supplant the causal relation between the absence of other motel security measures and the plaintiff's assault.

Peterson v. San Francisco Community College Dist., 36 Cal.3d 799, 685 P.2d 1193, 205 Cal.Rptr. 842 (1984).

Peterson was the victim of an attempted rape when using the stairwell of the parking garage. Similar attacks had occurred previously and was aggravated by heavy growth of bushes near the stairwells. The trial court dismissed the case due to a lack of factual issues because the school district owed no duty to the plaintiff. The California Supreme Court reversed and held that since the plaintiff was a registered student who paid tuition and paid parking lot fees that she was an invitee of the college and therefore a a special relationship and a duty of care between the parties did exist. The case was remanded for trial.

Rodriguez v. Inglewood Unified School Dist., 186 Cal.App.3d 707, 230 Cal.Rptr. 823 (1986).

Action was brought against school district for injuries inflicted by nonstudent on school grounds. A student was knifed on a campus where the plaintiff alleged had a long history of violent assaults upon students. No effort was made on the part of the school district to make the campus safe. The trial court sustained the school district's demurrer, and the plaintiff appealed. The Court of Appeal held that: (1) a special relationship existed between the student and school district so as to impose an affirmative duty on school district to protect student from injuries inflicted by nonstudent on school grounds; (2) the school district's failure to prevent injuries was not a dangerous condition of public property and did not impose statutory liability on the school district; and (3) no other constitutional or statutory provisions created mandatory duty on the part of the school district to prevent injuries and did not impose statutory liability on the school district. The judgment was affirmed.

Rowland v. Christian, 443 P.2d 561, 70 Cal.Rptr. 97 (1968).

Action was sustained by social guest of tenant when knob of cold water faucet in apartment broke while he was using it. A tenant complained to her apartment lessors that the cold water faucet was cracked and should be replaced. A guest of the tenant using the defective faucet severed tendons and nerves of his hand. The plaintiff claimed that tenant knew of a dangerous condition that existed and failed to warn or repair the condition that caused his injury. The trial court granted summary judgment and the plaintiff appealed. The supreme Court held: (1) that the proper test to be applied to liability of possessor of land is whether he acted as a reasonable man in view of probability of injuries to others; (2) plaintiff's status as trespasser, licensee, or invitee is not determinative; and (3) that issue as to whether tenant had been negligent in failing to warn of a non-obvious defect which had not been remedied by tenant was presented, precluding summary judgment for tenant.

Samson v. Saginaw Professional Bldg., 224 N.W.2d 843, 393 Mich. 393, 44 Mich.App. 658 (1975).

Action was brought by an employee of an office building tenant against the landlord for injuries sustained when attacked in the elevator by a mental patient. The patient was undergoing treatment at a state mental clinic which was also a building tenant. The patient pushed the emergency stop button and pulled a knife on the plaintiff. After robbing and stabbing the plaintiff her assailant fled. The jury awarded damages to the plaintiff and the landlord appealed. The appellate court affirmed the judgment finding that a duty existed on the part of the landlord and that he had sufficient knowledge to require further investigation into the type of patient's likely to visit the clinic and their propensity to be violent.

Schultz v. Elm Beverage Shoppe, 533 N.E.2d 349, 40 Ohio St.3d 326 (1988).

Schultz entered a liquor store during the course of a robbery. The store clerk shouted to the customer, "Run, run, call the cops." As Shultz turned to run he was shot. The robber shot and killed the clerk and shot Shultz again on the way out of the store. Shultz sued the clerk and the liquor store for the negligent act of the employee during the robbery. The trial court dismissed the case. The appellate court upheld that decision and stated that the clerk's conduct was reasonable in light of the urgency of the situation, his acts were privileged and therefore the store could not be liable for the injuries sustained by Shultz during the robbery.

Schwartz v. Helms Bakery Ltd., 67 Cal.2d 232, 430 P.2d 68, 60 Cal.Rptr. 510 (1967).

Action was brought against a bakery truck driver and owner on behalf of a four-year-old child who was injured while crossing the street in the middle of the block to buy a doughnut from a retail bakery truck. The child chasing the truck on foot ran across a public street nearly being struck by oncoming cars. The bakery truck driver who observed this close call directed the boy to go home to get a dime and meet him down the street at his next stop, saying nothing about safety to the boy. Upon return the boy once again darted out into the street to reach the truck and was struck by an oncoming car. The trial court granted a motion for nonsuit on behalf of the defendant. The plaintiff appealed. The Supreme Court held that there was a triable question of whether the owner and driver had discharged their duty to exercise ordinary care for the child who had been invited to be a customer of the business and to avoid creation of unreasonable risks of foreseeable harm and, if so, whether such breach proximately caused the injury to child. In addition, when the bakery truck driver told the boy that he would wait up the street, he had undertaken to direct the conduct of the child when he invited the boy to become a customer. At this point the driver entered into a legal relationship with the child and created a duty to exercise ordinary care for his safety.

Sheerin v. Holin Co., Supreme Ct. (Iowa 1986). The court reversed the trial court's decision to grant summary judgment in a lawsuit against an employer brought by the family of an employee who was stabbed to death by another employee. A waitress in a motel was raped and stabbed to death during business hours by the cook of the motel. Summary judgment was initially granted on the ground that worker's compensation provided the exclusive remedy. The Supreme Court stated that the term "In the course of employment" used to argue the worker's compensation motion may be defective if, "the employee deviates sufficiently from the line of duty so that his or her actions are foreign to the employer's work."

Small v. McKennan Hosp., 403 N.W.2d 410 (S.D. 1987).

Hospital's invitee was raped and murdered after being abducted from hospital parking lot. Supreme Court held that victim's estate did not have to prove occupier's knowledge of prior similar acts and that its liability would be determined by the "totality of circumstances."

Southland Corp. v. Superior Court, 203 Cal.App.3d 656 (1988).

The owners of a convenience store petitioned for a writ of mandate, claiming they had no duty, as a matter of law, to a customer injured after he had left their property, when he was attacked by unknown persons on a vacant and unpaved lot that was adjacent to the store, on his way back to this car after making purchases at the store. The plaintiff alleged that he and other customers frequently use the adjacent lot to park due to the limited space in front of the 7-Eleven store. On the day of his assault he and a friend saw juveniles loitering on the side of the store upon entering and were attacked by three "punk-rocker" types as they exited and were just ten feet off the property. The defendants acknowledged that they allow and encourage customers to park in the adjacent lot even though they do not own or lease the vacant property. The defendants were denied their motion for summary judgment and petitioned for a writ of mandate. The Court of Appeal denied the writ, holding: (1) a business proprietor clearly owes a duty of care to his customers whom he invites upon his land, and that the duty may extend to property over which he exercises actual or apparent control even if not owned or possessed; (2) that there was evidence that the defendants received a commercial advantage from the adjacent property, which apparently they had a leasehold right to use, and which use they at least passively encouraged; (3) their business was itself the attraction for both customers and loiterers; (4) that an issue of fact remained to be resolved with respect to the foreseeability of harm to the victim, even though no prior criminal assaults had ever occurred on the store premises

Sovary v. Los Angeles Police Department, 86 Cal.App.2d. 361 (1986).

A police agency may be held liable for an injury in a shopping center which they promised to patrol and which they advised against hiring private security. The court stated that citizens can sue the police for failure to protect them from crime if they relied on police promises to patrol, if the actions of the police increased their risk of harm. The police in this case withdrew their patrol shortly after advising the merchants not to hire private security and thereby increased the danger because of no patrol.

Taylor v. Hocker, 101 Ill.App.3d 639, 57 Ill.Dec. 112, 428 N.E.2d 662 (1981).

Customers brought action against shopping mall owners for injuries from an assault by a third person in the mall's parking lot. The plaintiff's were approached by an assailant who requested a ride. When they refused the stranger became violent and began the stab them with a knife. The plaintiff alleged failure to provide adequate lighting, failure to warn of the danger in the parking lot. The shopping center was paid common area maintenance charges by the mall tenants, part of which was used to hire security guards to patrol the common areas including the parking lots. The plaintiff produced evidence of prior property crimes and one violent crime prior to the opening of the mall. The trial court granted summary judgment in favor of the shopping mall. The plaintiff appealed. The Appellate Court held that: (1) owners' knowledge of shoplifting and thefts on the premises was not sufficient to give rise to a duty to protect customers from such assaults; and (2) the fact that owners had agreed to provide security personnel under the terms of their leases with store owners could not be construed as a voluntary undertaking to protect all shopping mall customers from criminal attack. The judgement was affirmed.

Ten Assocs. v. Brunsen, 492 So.2d 1149 (Fla. 1986).

Tenants brought action for damages where minor was abducted, taken into one of many unlocked and vacant units, and raped. The Florida District Court of Appeals held that even security measures proven to be inadequate and warranting compensatory liability may suffice to ward off a claim for punitive damages.

Trentacost v. Brussel, 412 A.2d 436 (N.J. 1980).

Tenant who was mugged in a hallway of an apartment house brought action against the landlord. A long term tenant was grabbed by the ankles at the top of the stairs and dragged from behind to the bottom of the stairs dislocating her shoulder, fracturing her ankle and jaw, and breaking teeth. The plaintiff alleged no lock on the common area front door which she and other tenants hd complained about for years. Evidence at produced at trial indicated 75 to 100 crimes in the neighborhood, including mostly burglaries and muggings. The apartment house was compared to the standard set by the local regulations for Multiple Dwellings which required locks on all access doors. The trial court entered judgment in favor of the plaintiff and the defendant appealed. The Supreme Court held: (1) evidence was sufficient to establish that landlord was negligent in failing to secure the entrance to common areas of building; (2) landlord could be found liable for criminal acts by third parties because of the warranty of habitability implied in the lease, independent of the foreseeability of the criminal act; and (3) landlord's violation of regulations constituted evidence of the landlord's negligence. The high crime rate in the immediate neighborhood was a factor in determining whether a criminal attack was foreseeable. Judgment was affirmed.

Urbano v. Days Inn of Am., 295 S.E.2d 240 (N.C. 1982).

A guest brought action for damages for injuries suffered in a parking lot assault. The North Carolina court found that the hotel had failed to use fences, had inadequate exterior lighting, had not retained private security patrols, and had generally failed to take reasonable security precautions.

Vermes v. American Dist. Tel. Co., 312 Minn. 33, 251 N.W.2d 101 (1977).

The court extended the duty of a landlord to inform a prospective tenant of qualities of the premises which might reasonably be undesirable from the tenant's point of view.

Vorbeck v. Carnegie's At Soulard, Inc., 704 S.W.2d 296 (Mo. 1986).

A woman was shot and robbed in a restaurant parking lot. Suit was filed against the restaurant and property owner for inadequate security. The case was dismissed and the appellate court upheld that 18 prior property crimes over three years did not place a duty to protect against third party criminal acts.

Waters v. New York City Hous. Auth., 116 A.D.2d 384, 501 N.Y.S.2d 385 (1986).

Action brought for a minor passerby who was robbed and sexually assaulted in a city housing project. A young girl was abducted from the sidewalk at knifepoint and was taken to a nearby building. The assailant gained access through an unlocked door. Evidence produced by the plaintiff showed that this door lock was broken for at least two years and that at least five previous crimes against tenant's occurred because of the broken door lock.. The plaintiff was taken to the roof via elevator and sexually assaulted and sodomized her. Summary judgment wad granted by the trial court. On appeal the Supreme Court held that: (1) the city housing authority had no duty to a passerby who was accosted at knife point by an unknown individual on a public street, compelled into an unlocked building in city housing authority project, and sexually assaulted in building, even though there had been a number of prior tenant complaints concerning broken front door lock and previous incidents occurring inside premises. The judgment was affirmed.

Weirum v. R.K.O. General, Inc., 539 P.2d 36, 15 Cal.3d 40, 123 Cal.Rptr. 468 (Sup. 1975). Action was brought for the wrongful death of a teenager who's vehicle was forced off the road by another radio listener. A "rock" radio station was conducting a contest to locate a popular disc jockey who would drive around area and award a cash prize to the first listener who would find him after receiving broadcasted clues of his location. During one broadcast listeners responding to hints, pursued the disc jockey at speeds up to 80 m.p.h. At a freeway off-ramp another responding vehicle forced the plaintiff's vehicle into the center divider causing it to overturn. Judgment was awarded to the plaintiff's decendants and the broadcaster appealed. The Supreme Court held that it was foreseeable that young radio listeners would race to arrive at the location of the disc jockey in order to receive a cash prize. Also, that a duty to control the conduct of third parties existed based upon the broadcaster's affirmative act of misfeasance creating an undue risk of harm. The judgment was affirmed.

Williams v. Office of Security & Intelligence, Inc., 509 So.2d 1282 (Fla. 1987).

Tenant brought action against contract security company for apartment complex when she was raped by another tenant. The plaintiff was raped by an intruder who broke into her apartment which was allegedly being protected by the defendant guard company. The guards were hired to patrol the apartment premises. Instead they slept, watched television, stayed in their apartments, socialized with their girlfriends, and left the premises. In addition the guards failed to prepare written incident reports or notify police of a series of rapes occurring at the complex. The trial court directed a verdict in favor of the defendants. The plaintiff appealed. The District Court of Appeal held that evidence was sufficient to support finding that the company hired to protect and guard apartment complex was negligent and that such negligence was proximate cause of rape of tenant. The judgment was reversed and remanded with directions.

Wingard v. Safeway Stores, Inc., 123 Cal.App.3d 37, 176 Cal.Rptr. 320 (1981).

A lawsuit was brought by an employee of a contract security guard service who was assigned to patrol a warehouse owned by the defendant. While on duty inside the warehouse guardshack the plaintiff was sexually assaulted by an unknown assailant who had gained access through an unlocked door. The plaintiff alleged inadequate security and for failure to prevent unauthorized entry into the building. Safeway was granted summary judgment by the court which held that they owed no duty to the plaintiff. On appeal the court affirmed the judgment stating that even though the warehouse was located in a high crime area, no prior similar acts of violence had been reported on the premises and that the owner is not bound to anticipate the criminal acts of third parties, especially where the assailant was a complete stranger and the criminal activity came about precipitously.

PROFESSIONAL ORGANIZATIONS AND RESOURCES

Academy of Security Educators & Trainers
4007 Arcade Court
Chesapeake Beach, MD 20732

American Academy of Forensic Sciences
225 South Academy Blvd., Suite A-201
Colorado Springs, CO 80910
(303) 596-6006

American Hotel & Motel Association
1407 South Harrison Road
East Lansing, Michigan 48823
(517) 353-5500

American National Standards Institute
1430 Broadway
New York, NY 10018
(212) 354-3300

American Society for Amusement Park Security
Cedar Point Amusement Park, Security Office
Sandusky, OH 44870

American Society for Industrial Security
1655 North Fort Meyer Drive, Suite 1200
Arlington, VA 22209
(703) 522-5800

American Society for Testing and Materials
1916 Race Street
Philadelphia, PA 19103
(215) 299-5400

American Society of Mechanical Engineers
345 East 47th Street
New York, NY 10017
(212) 705-7051

American Standards Testing Bureau
2525 Hyperion Avenue
Los Angeles, CA 90027
(213) 661-6900

American Standards Testing Bureau
40 Water Street
New York, NY 10004
(212) 943-3156

Associated Locksmiths of America, Inc.
3003 Live Oak Street
Dallas, TX 75204

Bank Administration Institute
60 Gould Center
Rolling Meadows, IL 60008
(312) 228-6200

Building Owners and Managers Association
1250 Eye Street, NW, Suite 200
Washington, DC 20005
(202) 289-7000

Bureau of Criminal Statistics
4949 Broadway
Sacramento, CA 94203
(California Crime Index)

Bureau of Justice Statistics
U.S Department of Justice
Washington, DC 20531
(National Crime Survey)

Canadian Society for Industrial Security
Box 8157, Postal Terminal
Ottawa, Ontario K1G 3H7, Canada

Canadian Society of Forensic Science
2660 Southvale Crecent, Suite 215-C
Ottawa, Ontario K1B4W5, Canada
(613) 731-2096

Federal Bureau of Investigation (FBI)
U.S. Department of Justice
Washington, DC 20535

Illumination Engineering Society
345 East 47th Street
New York, NY 10017
(212) 705-7926

International Association for Hospital Security
P.O. Box 637
Lombard, IL 60148

International Association for Shopping Center Security
2830 Clearview Place, NE, Suite 300
Atlanta, GA 30340
(404) 457-3575

International Association of Campus Law Enforcement
Administrators
P.O. Box 98127
Atlanta, GA 30359

International Association of Chiefs of Police, Inc.
13 Firstfield Road
Gaithersburg, MD 20878
(301) 948-0922

International Association of Professional Security Consultants
835 Deltona Blvd., Suite 77
Deltona, FL 32725
(904) 789-7878

International Conference of Building Officials
5360 South Workman Mill Road
Whittier, CA 90601
(213) 699-0541
(Uniform Building Code)

International Council of Shopping Centers
665 Fifth Avenue
New York, NY 10022
(212) 421-8181

National Council on Crime & Delinquency
77 Maiden Lane
San Francisco, CA 94108
(415) 956-5651

National Criminal Justice Association
444 N. Capitol Street, NW, Suite 608
Washington, DC 20001
(202) 347-4900

National Forensic Center
17 Temple Terrace, Suite 401
Lawrenceville, NJ 08648
(800) 526-5177

National Institute of Justice
U.S. Department of Justice
Washington, DC 20531
(Various crime studies)

National Safety Council
444 North Michigan Avenue
Chicago, IL 60611
(312) 527-4800

Nautical Almanac Office
United States Naval Observatory
Washington, DC 20390
(Sunrise/Sunset Tables)

Retail Security Association of Northern California
P.O. Box 96
Fremont, CA 94537
(415) 782-6841

The American Institute of Architects
1735 New York Avenue, NW
Washington, DC 20006

U.S. Government Printing Office
Superintendent of Documents
Washington, DC 20402
(Uniform Crime Reports)

Underwriters Laboratories (UL)
333 Pfingsten Road
Northbrook, IL 60062
(312) 272-8800

California Expert Witness Guide
Raoul D. Kennedy, Esq.
California Continuing Education of the Bar
2300 Shattuck Avenue, Suite 142
Berkeley, CA 94704
(415)642-6810 or (213)825-5301

*Depositions, Expert Witnesses and Demonstrative Evidence in
Personal Injury Cases*
David G. Miller
Practicing Law Institute
810 Seventh Avenue
New York, NY 10019
(212)765-5700

Expert Witness Checklists
Douglas Danner
Lawyers Co-operative Publishing Co.
Aqueduct Building, Suite 660
Rochester, NY 14694
(716)546-5530

Expert Witness Handbook
Tips and Techniques for the Litigation Consultant
Dan Poynter
Para Publishing
P.O. Box 4232-M
Santa Barbara, CA 93140
(805)968-7277

Forensic Bibliography
National Forensic Center
17 Temple Terrace, Suite 401
Lawrenceville, NJ 08648
(800)526-5177 or (609)883-0550

Guide To Experts' Fees
National Forensic Center
17 Temple Terrace, Suite 401
Lawrenceville, NJ 08648
(800)526-5177 or (609)883-0550

Jury Trials, The Phychology of Winning Strategy
Donald E. Vinson
The Mitchie Company
P.O. Box 7587-B
Charlottesville, VA 22906
(800)446-3410

Lawyers Desk Reference
Techical Sources for Conducting a Personal Injury Action
Harry M. Philo, Esq.
Lawyers Co-0perative Publishers Company
Aqueduct Building, Suite 660
Rochester, NY 14694
(716)546-5530

and

Bancroft-Whitney Company
301 Brannan Street, Suite 421
San Francisco, CA 94107
(415)986-4410

Preparing Witnesses for Trial
California Continuing Education of the Bar
2300 Shattuck Avenue, Suite 142
Berkeley, CA 94704
(415)642-6810 or (213)825-5301

The Expert Witness
Peter Dorram
Planners Press
1313 East 60th Street
Chicago, IL 60637
(312)955-9100

The Expert Witness in Litigation
Hirsh and Pemberton
Defense Research Institute
750 North Lake Shore Drive
Chicago, IL 60611
(312)944-0575

Using Experts in Civil Cases
Melvin D. Kraft
Practicing Law Institute
810 Seventh Avenue
New York, NY 10019
(212)765-5700

What Makes Juries Listen
Sonya Hamlin
Prentis-Hall, Law & Business
855-D Valley Road
Clifton, NJ 07013
(201) 472-7400

PERIODICALS

ABA Journal
American Bar Association
750 North Lake Shore Drive
Chicago, IL 60611

California Lawyer
State Bar Association of California
1016 Fox Plaza, 1390 Market Street
San Francisco, CA 94102
(415)558-9888

Canadian Security
1880 O'Connor Drive, Suite 303
Toronto, Ontario M4A 2P1
Canada

CTLA Forum
California Trial Lawyers Association
1020 12th Street, 4rd Floor
Sacramento, CA 95814
(916)442-6902

Hawaii Bar News
Hawaii State Bar Association
Pacific Tower, 1001 Bishop Street, Suite 950

Honolulu, HI 96813
(808)537-1868

Journal of Security Administration
London House Press
1550 Northwest Highway
Park Ridge, IL 60068

San Francisco Attorney
Bar Association of San Francisco
685 Market Street, Suite 700
San Francisco, CA 94105
(415)764-1600

Security
1350 E. Touhy Avenue
Des Plaines, IL 60018
(312)635-8800

Security Management
American Society for Industrial Security
1655 North Fort Meyer Drive
Arlington, VA 22209
(703)522-5800

Security Systems Administration
101 Crossways Park
Woodbury, NY 11797

Security World
P.O. Box 5080
Des Plaines, IL 60018

The Advocate
Los Angeles Trial Lawyers Association
2140 West Olympic Blvd.
Los Angeles, CA 90015

The Campus Law Enforcement Journal
P.O. Box 98127
Atlanta, GA 30359

The Expert and the Law
National Forensic Center
17 Temple Terrace, Suite 401
Lawrenceville, NJ 08648
(800)526-5177

The Verdict
The Association of Southern California Defense Counsel
123 Truxtun Avenue
Bakersfield, CA 93301
(805)325-7124

Trial Lawyers Forum
Texas Trial Lawyers Association
1220 Colorado
Austin, TX 78701
(512)476-3852

Trial Magazine
Association of Trial Lawyers of America
1050 31st Street NW
Washington, DC 20007
(202)965-3500

NEWSLETTERS

Corporate Security
87 Terminal Drive
Plainview, NY 11803

Hospital Security and Safety Management
Hotel/Motel Security and Safety Management
Nursing Home Security and Safety Management

Rusting Publications
403 Main Street
Port Washington, NY 11050
(516)883-1440

IAPSC Newsletter
International Assn. of Professional Security Consultants
835 Deltona Blvd., Suite 77
Deltona, FL 32725
(904)789-7878

Private Security Case Law Reporter
Strafford Publications, Inc.
1375 Peachtree Street, N.E., Suite 235
Atlanta, GA 30367
(404)881-1141

Security Law Newsletter
Crime Control Research Corporation
1063 Thomas Jefferson St. N.W.
Washington DC, 20007
(202)337-2700

Security Letter
166 East 96th Street
New York, NY 10028

Security Systems Digest
7820 Little River Turnpike
Annandale, VA 22003

The Expert Witness Reporter
P.O. Box 1093
Columbia, MD 21044

COLOPHON

This book was produced with computerized equipment and desktop publishing software. A word processor was used to organize the initial research information as well as to write, edit, and set type for this book.

PRODUCTION NOTES

Input:	Computer - Leading Edge, Model D2 (AT)
	Word Processor - Microsoft Word, 4.0
	Desktop Publishing - Ventura Publisher, 2.0
Output:	Hewlett Packard LaserJet, Series II
Typefaces:	Text - Times Roman & Helvetica
	Cover - Garamond
Cover Art:	Lou-Anne Fauteck, Aegis Books, Oakland, CA
Mechanical:	David Brostoff & Associates, Berkeley, CA
Paper:	Text - 60 lb. publishers white
	Cover - 12 pt., C1S white
Ink:	Text - standard black
	Cover - three-color with plastic laminate
Printing:	Offset lithography (web press)
	McNaughton & Gunn, Ann Arbor, Michigan
Binding:	Perfect Bound
Edition:	First, 2000 copies